ARCHITECTURE
A CRASH
COURSE

ARCHITECTURE
A CRASH
COURSE
HILARY FRENCH

WATSON-GUPTILL
PUBLICATIONS

New York

First published in the United States in 1998 by
Watson-Guptill Publications, a division of BPI
Communications, Inc., 1515 Broadway, New York, NY 10036

Library of Congress Catalog Card Number: 98-86082

ISBN 0-8230-0976-9

This book was conceived, designed, and produced by
THE IVY PRESS LIMITED
2/3 St Andrews Place
Lewes, East Sussex, BN7 1UP

Art Director: PETER BRIDGEWATER
Designer: JANE LANAWAY
Editorial Director: SOPHIE COLLINS
Commissioning Editor: VIV CROOT
Page layout: CHRIS LANAWAY, TRUDI VALTER
Picture research: LIZ EDDISON
Illustrations: KAREN DONNELLY and IVAN HISSEY

Printed in Hong Kong

1 2 3 4 5 6 7 8 9 10/06 05 04 03 02 01 00 99 98

DEDICATION

*For my daughter Jessie,
and for Nicholas.*

Contents

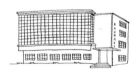

Introduction

Many histories of architecture have attempted to explain why buildings look the way they do. Some are works of detection, unraveling the secrets of the past. Many are written as "stories" with a beginning, a middle, and an end somewhere in twentieth-century modernism.

This book is less like an explanation and more like a description —a survey of the past—with no plot and no storyline. It uses conventional categories and stylistic classifications that can be found in histories of art to sort the architects and various buildings into a roughly chronological order. Rather than including vernacular or traditional buildings, it is

The Erectheion (421–406 B.C.), on the Acropolis in Athens, Greece.

The stepped pyramid of Zoser at Saqqara in Egypt.

focused on the work of architects, and includes their theoretical or "unbuilt works," either writings or drawings. Wherever possible well-known buildings are used to illustrate the different styles or categories.

Architecture can be seen as a response to the primary human need for shelter (and comfort). Different cultures have all produced different kinds of buildings. Variations in climate initially, and later in religious beliefs and economic

The church of San Giorgio Maggiore in Venice, Italy (designed 1565, built 1602–10), by Andrea Palladio.

External escalators on the façade of the CNAC, Paris, France (1971–74), by Piano and Rogers.

systems, resulted in different "traditional" or vernacular buildings, using the most easily available local materials. Learning about such vernacular architecture and the ritual of everyday life that it houses is a fundamental part of our understanding of the human condition.

Architecture can also be many other things. Architecture as "Art" with a capital A considers itself to be something more than mere building. Architecture as history illustrates the power of the institutions, namely the state, the crown, or the church, with their enduring, preserved monuments,

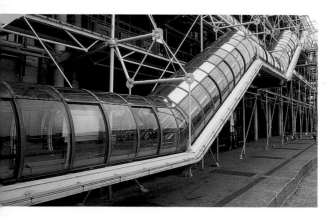

Asides
Here, the author takes a breather and engages you with tidbits about the subject matter and architects being discussed. Maybe they are overrated? Or maybe their new ideas were, or are, a revolutionary mode of architectural thinking? Read on and find out.

The Guggenheim Museum in Bilbao, Spain (1998), by Frank Gehry.

their castles, palaces, and cathedrals. Architecture might also be physical proof of scientific achievement, of technological progress, with the tallest buildings and widest spans. On a domestic scale, ordered and well-serviced living spaces might be seen as representative of a highly evolved civilization.

Whatever its cultural claims, most architectural history tends to deal only with the visual—that is, with the way buildings look—in preference to all the pragmatic functional issues of buildings, their construction, or how they are used. The words and pictures here can attempt to evoke what the sensual

The Empire State Building in Manhattan, New York (1929–31), by Shreve, Lamb, and Harman.

experience might be. To understand even one building fully it is necessary to learn something of the culture that produced it. This survey is only the first step, encouraging you to recognize

Radio City Music Hall in New York; true 1930s Art Deco.

and understand some of the basics of form and structure, and of light and decoration, together with something of the ideas and intentions of the people who designed them.

Reading architectural history can seem like a catalog of revivals with occasional startling interruptions as something new appears. The progression from one style to another can only be a matter of guesswork. On one hand, architecture, like any practical craft, looks to the past for tried and trusted construction methods and familiar and comfortable imagery; on the other, it yearns for originality, and looks to the future, the daring and excitement of the new.

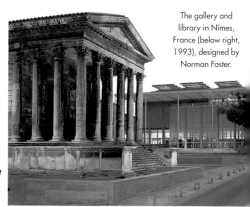

The gallery and library in Nîmes, France (below right, 1993), designed by Norman Foster.

While society is now more complex and expectations of architecture are higher, the requirement remains unchanged; as W. R. Lethaby said in his book Architecture, Mysticism and Myth *almost 100 years ago,* "Great art is not a question of shapes and appearances which may be copied, it is fine response to noble requirement; a living architecture is always being hurled forward from change to change."

One of the Art Nouveau métro entrances in Paris, France (1899–1904), designed by Hector Guimard.

Architecture belongs to everybody. Unlike painting or music, which can be avoided or denied, the history of architecture, the enduring remains of the past, is all around us. Our experience of architecture is of the buildings, the everyday spaces of towns and cities, that frame the lives of ordinary people.

HILARY FRENCH

3100 B.C. Menes conquers the Delta Kingdom of Lower Egypt and unifies the country under one crown. The capital is established at Memphis.

3000–2800 B.C. Canal construction begins in Egypt; flutes and tambourines in use for ceremonial bands.

2400–2200 B.C. The upright weaving loom introduced in Egypt; before this, cloth had been woven on horizontal looms pegged to the ground.

3400~900 B.C.

Pyramid Power
The Egyptians

Stepped pyramid of King Zoser.

The pyramids, gigantic, anonymous, and impersonal, were arguably the first examples of monumental architecture. Built in durable stone to last forever, they are symbolic of the importance the Egyptians placed on the afterlife: the timeless significance of the soul compared to the temporary nature of the body.

The earliest pyramids are stepped, such as the pyramid of King Zoser at Saqqara, and were superseded by the later ones where the stepped construction is filled in to give a smooth finish. The highest is the pyramid of Cheops at Giza, with two burial chambers, a wide gallery, and several air shafts. Temples, generally rectangular in plan, were also built as permanent structures of cut stone with column and lintel (trabeated) structures, and columns in regular grids. Typically the tops of the columns (capitals) are carved to look like palm leaves, imitating simple houses made of lotus plants, reeds, and canes that are plentiful along the banks of the Nile River. The entrance was through a bastion or pylon with battered (inclined) walls, via a courtyard. Often the only visible elevation, the approach was lined with sphinxes.

The hypostyle (many-pillared) hall at the Great Temple of Amman, Karnak, dating from 1530–323 B.C.

KARNAK AND LUXOR

Little remains of the buildings of the Middle Kingdom, but the New Kingdom (1570–1085 B.C.) saw some spectacular temple buildings. At Karnak and Luxor there are vast halls with a multitude of papyrus columns, and clerestories to let light in at a high level.

2000 B.C. Egyptians invent the shaduf, a device for raising water avoiding unpleasant stooping; it's so good it's still in use today.

1360–1280 B.C. Tutankhamen buried in his tomb amid great splendor.

1190 B.C. Rameses III repels the invading Sea People, marauding bandits from the eastern Mediterranean and Caspian Sea.

The Great Temple at Abu Simbel has a pylon façade with statues over 65 feet high. Many temples of traditional form, such as the temple of Horus at Edfu and the temple of Isis at Philae (280–50 B.C.), survive from the Ptolemaic period, established following the breakup of Alexander the Great's empire.

N is for...

Napoleon Bonaparte (1769–1821), emperor of France and first modern demagogue, knew a good thing when he saw one. Though Egyptian forms were known in France before the French Revolution of 1789, Boney discovered the pyramid and the obelisk for himself while on his Egyptian campaign of 1798, and was particularly smitten with the latter (as monuments to himself, naturally, embossed or carved with the ubiquitous "N"s). The new emperor soon graduated to the Imperial Roman style for the many monuments he would leave around Europe, and thereby set a standard. Of a kind. The pyramid? Napoleon would have been interested in the glass one erected in the courtyard of the Paris Louvre in 1986 ...

NAMES ON THE WALL

*Although little is known about architects at this period, we know that it was **Imhotep**, architect and minister of **King Zoser**, who was responsible for the first known pyramid at Saqqara in Egypt. Attribution was not always so straightforward, however. An inscription at Edfu tells us that the plan of the pyramid at Giza was divinely inspired. But in a nice twist, Imhotep was himself later worshiped as a god in Lower Egypt. In the twentieth century, Egyptian architect **Hassan Fathy** (1900–1989) has achieved recognition for his work in the revival of vernacular building techniques, including sun-dried brick, and the use of passive cooling systems, and in his concern for providing for the poor.*

The three famous Fourth Dynasty pyramids at Giza, near Cairo, are the finest "true" pyramids.

Mykerinos

Chephren

Cheops

800–750 B.C. The *Iliad* and the *Odyssey*, Greek classics, are written; they may be by Homer, who may be one or more persons and who may or may not have come from Asia Minor.

750–700 B.C. Bards go professional in Greece and accompany themselves on lyres.

580–540 B.C. Black figure pottery reaches perfection; most scenes are mythological in subject, and some are pornographic.

850~297 B.C.

Temples and Other Erectheions
Greek and Hellenistic

The enduring beauty of ancient Greek buildings is rarely disputed. They show an assertive simplicity of form, scale related to human occupation, and decoration related to material and construction. The

The Ionic Erectheion (421–406 B.C.) on the Acropolis replaced the temple of Athena destroyed during the Persian invasion. Caryatids support the roof over the porch on the south façade.

relationship to nature is also of great importance, with buildings seemingly occurring naturally, and theaters carved into the ground. The importance given to the spaces between the buildings, such as the agora for civic, commercial, and philosophical interchange, implies that social structures were as important as the physical structures of the city.

The surviving stone buildings use the same trabeated structures that were used for timber buildings. Early construction methods—mud-brick walls with timber posts to support timber lintels and beams—produced very simple logical structures. For important buildings, such as temples, timbers were gradually replaced with stone. The classic temples vary in size but use the same formal elements and are variations on the basic theme of a rectangular enclosed space with a colonnaded porch (portico) at one end. The most complex have several rooms inside, porches at both ends, and ambulatories at the sides with a double row

of columns. The stonework was often covered with a plaster or stucco, and painted and gilded with a common color scheme. Bright blue was used for triglyphs and cornice blocks, red for spaces between the cornice blocks and bands, blue with gold stars for the ceiling panels, and gilt bronze for figures.

The type of column and frieze used also varies. The different styles are known as the Orders. The Doric order, named after the Dorian people of mainland Greece, is the earliest. Columns are chunky, fluted, and tapering toward the top, with a simple square capital and no base. The Ionic order developed in the Aegean Islands and the

c 387 B.C. Plato founds the Academy in Athens where the jeunesse dorée of Athenian aristocracy learn to philosophize.

350 B.C. The sculptor Praxiteles produces the Venus of Cnidus, the first-known female nude.

220–180 B.C. The Greeks introduce town planning; chaotic marketplaces at Ephesus and Miletus are knocked down and replaced with serene squares.

NAMES ON THE WALL

The Greeks were the originators of the term "architect" and possibly also the first to apply contractual penalties. A law enacted at Ephesus stated that if an architect's "extras" exceeded the contract amount by more than 25%, he was held personally liable for them. The Greeks sought eternally valid rules of form and proportion but were not without their critics. **Hermogenes,** *architect and foremost Hellenistic architectural theorist, threw a tantrum part way through building one temple and abandoned the Doric for the Ionic, saying that "the distribution of the triglyphs and metopes is troublesome and inharmonious." Sigh...*

coast of Asia Minor. The column is generally more slender and finely fluted, has a capital cut from a rectangular block, and is raised on a square base. The capital is carved to form volutes on each side. The Doric and Ionic orders were used for most of the finest surviving temples.

The Doric Parthenon (447–436 B.C.) is the principal building on the Acropolis in Athens.

HELLENISTIC

The Corinthian order, invented in Athens in the fifth century B.C., with more flamboyant capitals of curling acanthus leaves, was little used at the time but became common much later, in the Hellenistic period of *ALEXANDER THE GREAT'S* (356–323 B.C.) empire. The Olympeion (174 B.C.–A.D. 131) is the earliest large-scale building using the Corinthian order. Alexander's empire also saw more regimented planning in cities, and the introduction of the abstract controlling device, the grid. Plans for Alexandria, Priene, and Miletus all included attention to the construction of vistas and monumental effects. Military design also developed, with the construction of defensive structures and fortifications.

Stylobate curves upward

Façade has eight columns

If you see it my way

The Greeks continually pursued perfection. Columns, if perfectly straight, would appear to be concave; if the horizontal lines of stylobates and cornices were horizontal, they would appear to sag in the middle. So they developed a system of optical corrections; columns generally bulge outward in the center to appear straight. The columns of the Parthenon also lean inward about 15 inches to counter the appearance of falling outward, and the stylobate gently curves upward to around 15 inches in the center of the ends and 28 inches in the center of the long sides.

44 B.C. Julius Caesar, declared a god by his own peers, is assassinated by his friend Brutus and other conspirators on the Ides (15th) of March.

30 A.D. Jesus of Nazareth crucified in Jerusalem.

330 The Roman emperor Constantine establishes his eastern capital, Constantinople (later Byzantium, then Istanbul).

509 B.C.~A.D. 1200

Empire Building
Rome and Byzantium

Pont du Gard aqueduct.

The domed interior of the Hagia Sophia, Istanbul (A.D. 532–37).

Taking over from the Etruscans, the Romans built an empire that started with a few Italian states and spread across most of Europe to the west and as far as the Persian Empire in the east. The Romans showed their domination through extensive lawmaking and the control of physical territory—building straight roads irrespective of natural features, and cities planned with ruthless grids.

The Roman forum, a rectilinear enclosed space containing and limiting the movement of people, was the antithesis of the Greek open space—a physical manifestation of the movement from democracy to imperium. The building techniques that enabled the Romans to dominate the landscape with viaducts, vast bathhouses, and civic buildings were very different also. Where the Greeks made use of columns and beams, the Romans favored walls. Built from bricks or small pieces of stone, walls could extend much higher and openings could be any size, with semicircular arches. In conjunction with concrete, massive structures could be achieved. The Classical orders, with variations, were employed in a decorative fashion, applied to the surface of masonry walls.

Count Your Blessings

Masons recruited in Byzantium by Vladimir I brought masonry building techniques and dome forms to Russia. The pyramidical forms continued with variations, but were generally characterized by domes, often on very elongated drums of massive masonry. The Cathedral of the Intercession, known as St. Basil's, in Red Square, Moscow, shows the same basic arrangement, with an eight-pointed star in plan, a tall central space encircled by an originally open corridor, and domed apses. The elaborate decorations and exotic onion domes were added in the seventeenth century.

EARLY CHRISTIAN, A.D. 200–400

Early Christian buildings date from around A.D. 200—catacombs, martyria (usually circular, built to mark sacred sites), and meeting houses for worship. Once Christianity was officially recognized as the religion of the Roman Empire in A.D. 391, the basilica was adopted as the model for

410 Rome sacked by Visigoths; the last Roman troops leave Britain.

425 The Mausoleum of Galla Placidia is built in Ravenna; its dark interior is enlivened by mosaics, showing how far the Byzantine influence had spread westward.

527 Justinian crowned emperor of the Eastern Roman Empire; with his empress, an ex-actress called Theodora, he inaugurates a glittering reign of political triumph, legislative acumen, and architectural splendor.

NAMES ON THE WALL

We know a lot about Roman architecture because of the extensive self-promotional writings of one **Vitruvius***. However, some doubts exist as to whether he was himself an architect. The emperor* **Hadrian***, on the other hand, almost certainly was, although told to "go away and paint pumpkins" by a jealous older rival,* **Apollonius of Damascus***. The removal of Apollonius's head after a second insult put paid to any further criticism. The Romans were responsible for the invention of concrete, building bylaws, multiseater stadia, and leisure complexes.*

imported but Eastern influence continued. Intellectual achievement, the harmony of proportions, and the intricacies of structure were considered equal to, if not more important than, emotive or sensual qualities. Hagia Sophia (532–37 B.C.), built by a mathematician, Anthemios, is the most spectacular building. In the middle Byzantine period (9th–12th century) symbolism expressed in paintings and mosaics required certain formal arrangements. The cross-in-square plan became a common type, with a central higher dome on a drum, often surrounded by lower smaller domes over apses on all sides.

churches. Originally a meeting hall, it was ideally suited to accommodate a congregation. Typically rectilinear in plan, it had a higher central nave lit by clerestory windows and flanked by colonnaded aisles. A curved end (apse), originally the judge's position, formed the place for the altar.

BYZANTINE, A.D. 400–1200

The emperor Constantine left home to establish a new capital at Byzantium (Constantinople) in A.D. 330. Classical motifs and Roman building techniques were

The Colosseum, Rome (A.D. 70–82), a typical Roman amphitheater with gladiatorial arena.

The upper story was added A.D. 222–24

Anything For a Party

As egos and Empire grew apace, so did the Roman Triumph, most famously awarded to victorious generals returning home—for example, the Arch of Titus in Rome's Forum, which celebrates and records the sack of Jerusalem by the future emperor in A.D. 70. But triumphalism was in full flow as early as the first century B.C., with temporary arches; later, permanent structures feature not only in Italy, but around the Roman world, with one- and three-doored examples testifying not only to the skills of architects, masons, and sculptors, but also to the great Roman pastime of blowing one's own trumpet.

800 Charlemagne, king of the Franks, is crowned Holy Roman Emperor by the Pope. He unites and reforms the Western Church and imposes the Benedictine Rule.

1066 William the Conqueror seizes the English throne and introduces the Norman building style (stone and round arches).

1096. The Cluniac orders begin to spread rapidly, and Gregorian chant echoes through the new ecclesiastical buildings appearing all over France.

700~1200

Heavy Duty

Romanesque and Norman

The term Romanesque was coined in the nineteenth century to describe buildings that continued Roman form and construction. A generalized term, it covers a long period of time and a wide geographical area. Stocky, chunky, solid, and primitive looking, Romanesque buildings are generally recognizable by their round arches. Exteriors and interiors are clearly related to each other.

Durham Cathedral (1093–1133) has alternating circular piers with grooved decoration.

begun by William the Conqueror, is typical of the exquisite churches of Normandy. It has two square towers on the west façade, rounded arches, and originally a timber roof construction.

Carolingian architecture is sometimes distinguished as a separate style from other Romanesque by its geographical location in France, Germany, and the Netherlands. It is named after Charlemagne, the Holy Roman Emperor from 800 A.D. He promoted a return to Constantine Christianity with basilican planning but with altered form: prominent towers, important ends both east and west, and the heavy, solid construction typical of the

SPOT
THE
STYLE

The meaning of Romanesque depends on where you come from. If those rounded arches seem to suggest clues, think again. The architectures of the French Channel coast and of Sicily don't seem to have much in common. One has its rounded arches, the other doesn't, yet the pundits call both "Romanesque." Norman factions held court for years in both places, and more besides. And to confuse matters, many a small church is diagnosed with a case of the Romanesque as severe as any big cathedral. Keep at it.

Neither powerful nor dominating, and without the grandeur of Roman buildings or the mystery of Byzantine architecture, although using elements from both, the Romanesque has a picturesque quality and a much "friendlier" feel. The Abbaye-aux-Hommes in Caen (1060–81),

1098 The Cistercian order is founded in Burgundy, France. By 1200 there will be more than 500 Cistercian abbeys in Europe.

1139 Alfonso Henriques, count of Portugal, calls himself king, and presses English crusaders into service to oust the Moors from Lisbon.

1334 Plague in Constantinople. Genoese traders spread the Black Death westward. Monks and town dwellers suffer most, living in close proximity, and this era of monastic buildings comes to an end.

Romanesque. The Palatine chapel at Aachen is the most dramatic building of the period.

In Italian Romanesque, the picturesque quality is evident; the tower (campanile) is detached from the main body of the church and external arcading is common. Pisa Cathedral (1063–1118; 1261–72) is the best known, with its leaning campanile with arcades at every level, as well as three more levels of arcades on the façade of the cathedral itself.

NORMAN

In England the Romanesque is called Norman, and starts with Westminster Abbey, built by Edward the Confessor. Almost every cathedral and abbey church was rebuilt at this time and, as well as the typical Romanesque, some had variations—Ely has a single west tower. Lincoln has niches on the façade. An exception to the usual timber roof structure, Durham Cathedral (1093–1133) has a rib-vaulted nave, which is one of the very earliest of such sophistication. The ruins of Fountains Abbey in Yorkshire (1157–1200) give the most complete picture of monastery building and life in the enclosed communities.

Castles were also enclosed communities. Norman castles had keeps on a raised mound (motte), often surrounded by a moat and an adjoining enclosure (bailey). Examples include the White Tower at London (1086–97) and Orford, Suffolk (1160–72).

Anything for a Quiet Life

The rigors of medieval monasticism, the magnificence of the monastery buildings, and the might of the monastic orders themselves make a bizarre combination. In Britain their remains have inspired artists of every kind. Try to imagine Wordsworth without Tintern Abbey, Turner without Byland, and the eighteenth-century Picturesque Movement without Fountains, Whitby, or Rievaulx. The peace of these places proclaims the faith and ability of their builders, and conceals three centuries of conflict between church and state.

Pisa Cathedral's famous leaning campanile (1174–1271), with its decorative arcades, is a less robust, finer version of the Romanesque.

1096 The First Crusade to the Holy Land sets out. Islam and Christianity confront each other.

1137 The flying buttress is invented. The buttresses carry the weight of the building structure, enabling walls to be thinner and windows to be inserted in them almost at will.

1144 Robert de Mont-Saint-Michel describes the building of Chartres: "... as if by magic towers rose into the air ... men and women could be seen ... singing of the miracle of the Lord ...."

1100~1250

Reaching for God
Gothic

Gothic cathedrals, with their great height and multiple flying buttresses, rise dramatically above the surrounding landscape, forming intricate openwork silhouettes against the sky. Inside, spaces seem similarly detached from the mere earthly, with the slenderest of columns rising to impossible heights and hazy daylight filtering through stained glass tracery and clerestory windows. The Gothic cathedrals represent a synthesis of God, Humanity, and Nature—the harmonious combination of religious symbolism with the most logical and efficient structures.

Narrow bays accentuate the verticality of the towers

The famous rose window is the backdrop to the statue of the virgin and child flanked by angels

The main part of the west front of Notre Dame in Paris was built in 1220–50.

Build 'em Big!
Size became a dominant feature of Gothic cathedral building. Amiens (1220–70) was large enough at more than 9,000 square yards to hold the entire city population. Strasbourg (1245–75) was as tall as a 40-story building. Beauvais, intended to be the largest, was never completed. Building started on the choir (158 feet/ 48 meters to the vault) in 1220, but by 1284 some of its vaulting had collapsed. The cathedral consists of the choir and transepts only; the proposed nave was never built.

The essence of Gothic building is its structure—the result of the combination of flying buttresses, pointed arches, and rib vaults. These elements work together to make a skeletal, cagelike structure with only the need for very thin, lightweight panels to fill the gaps (infill panels). As well as allowing greater spans through vastly reduced material weight, arches and rib vaults group all the vertical loads (weight of the building) into single points, so columns can be used. Flying buttresses, detached at the end of bridge-like arches, take the lateral loads. Solid, load-bearing walls are redundant and the space between the columns can be filled with windows. Similarly, every other element has a useful role to play. In what is effectively a linear

1174 The French William of Sens supervises the rebuilding of Canterbury Cathedral. He is severely injured in a fall from the scaffolding.

1180 France becomes home to the first windmill in the western world.

1226 Louis IX (Saint Louis) ascends the throne. Paris and its university become the center of intellectual Christendom.

structure, the ends are contained and supported at the east end by the apse, like an arch on its side, and at the west end by a pair of square towers that contain entrance porches. The pinnacles, pointing skyward on the buttresses, add weight to tie the buttresses to the ground. Spires act as landmarks and allow the sound of bells to be heard far away.

Spain

Gothic cathedrals are not as common in Spain as in Northern Europe. Seville Cathedral (1402–1519) is a particularly unusual late Gothic building. It was built on the foundations of a mosque, giving it an enormous square plan, which was neatly gothicized by doubling up the side aisles. It is a curious mixture of the Christian and Moorish. The orange tree court, the original forecourt for ritual ablutions, is a curious entrance space and the bell tower is a converted minaret. The famous Mesquita at Cordoba, with endless Moorish horseshoe-shaped arches, was also converted to Christian uses in the thirteenth century with the insertion of a Gothic section.

Vaulting. Bridge that Gap!

Rib vaulting was a dramatic innovation. With the barrel vaulting of the Romanesque and earlier, the wider the space, the higher the vault, the heavier the load. Vertical load was carried on continuous solid walls which had to become buttressed to take any increase in load. Rib vaulting removes all the superfluous material and weight. Ribs gather the vertical loads onto columns, rather than walls. The buttresses, like an additional row of columns, are detached —the characteristic flying buttresses. Later, more ornate vaults were called "fans."

Fan vaulting.

SYMBOLISM

The building of the great Gothic cathedrals coincided with a change in belief away from blind faith and away from the idea of God as an unknown fearsome force that was associated with the dark and mysterious churches. God is now visible—man is created in his image and nature is his kingdom. The building tells the story. No longer anonymous, the saints and apostles can now be

identified, carved in the door surrounds, and depicted in murals. Forests of tall columns rising up into branches of rib vaults are an imitation of nature. The transepts, which break up the linearity of the nave, provide lateral support and give it the Latin cross plan. The great interior space contains music and the rising clouds of incense. High above the nave, clerestory windows light the vault of Heaven and huge windows of colored glass tell stories in light. The individual is recognizably insubstantial in relationship to the vast and complex entity of the cathedral.

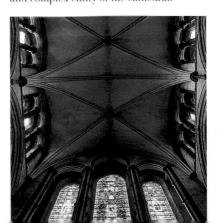

The introduction of rib vaulting meant spaces became higher and higher.

1202 Mathematician Leonardo da Pisa (aka Fibonacci) writes *Liber Abaci*, introducing arabic numerals to Christendom.

1291 Clear glass invented in Venice. The window is born.

1300 Sulfuric acid discovered by the modest alchemist known only as False Geber.

1200~1450

Being God
Gothic 2

SPOT THE STYLE

Gothic is probably the best-known architectural style of Europe, identified with its cathedrals, their rib vaults and flying buttresses, their galleries and large clerestory windows. But watch out. Some of these features existed before the 1200s in other places. It's so confusing. Pundits nod at the Abbey of St. Denis as the earliest complete Gothic building, but the style developed in different ways everywhere. In England look no further than Canterbury Cathedral, and for a fusion of French and German styles see Cologne Cathedral. Tread warily.

The stained-glass rose window.

Gothic cathedrals exist in the greatest numbers in France and England, though the French cathedral builders attempted more daring structures than their English counterparts. They built much higher naves, often with several tiers inside; several levels of flying buttresses, and fleches *rather than towers over the crossing. In plan the French cathedrals include* chevet *East ends, usually with radiating chapels.*

The earliest Gothic building is the rebuilding of the choir of the Abbey of Saint Denis near Paris (1140), with a seven-bay chevet end. Notre Dame de Paris (1163) is archetypal French Gothic. It is enormously high (105 feet/32 meters), with three levels of flying buttresses, double aisles, and a chevet end with chapels. The west front has two square towers and circular windows. The pilgrimage church at Chartres (1194– c.1220) is the most popular. The west towers and nave are part of an earlier (1135–60) building destroyed by fire. In order to accommodate large crowds it has huge transepts, including very wide aisles with triple portals at both sides.

The thirteenth-century Rayonnant style, developed in France as a reaction to the vast scale of the cathedrals, produced much smaller-scale churches. The Sainte Chapelle in Paris (1243) is a particularly beautiful space: a simple rectangle with an apsidal east end and spectacular stained-glass work intended to be seen close up. Externally the small building is covered with pinnacles and spires.

A Chip off the Old Block?

Visit any of the great Gothic cathedrals of Europe and virtually the first thing you see are statues in niches at the west door, and frequently around the outside. The themes? Prophets, apostles, and saints with crisply pleated robes or, for the adventurous, Bible stories such as Jacob's Dream (on the west front of Bath Abbey), every scheme arranged to a theological plan. Some were even painted. In the thirteenth century, sculpture originally had the status of the icing on the cake, the province of a master craftsman, but by the fifteenth century the gilt had faded a little and the sculptor now mingled with the masons as one of the boys.

1381 Wat Tyler and Jack Cade lead the Peasant's Revolt in England. The class system does not budge.

1387 German craftsmen rebuild Milan Cathedral in the Northern Gothic style.

1415 The Duc de Berry commissions 12 castles and an illustrated book to show them off: *Les Très Riches Heures du Duc de Berry* by the Limbourg brothers.

ENGLAND

The Gothic period covers more than three centuries and it is usual for the style to be further divided. In England the period is roughly divided by century, generally related to the complexity of the tracery. The thirteenth-century "Early English" is sometimes called "Lancet" to describe the simple pointed windows before complex tracery was established. Canterbury Cathedral's Trinity Chapel is a good example. Westminster Abbey was largely rebuilt between 1245 and 1269 in the Early English style, with this specific style used again in the late fourteenth century to extend the nave. "Decorated" is the next phase, roughly fourteenth century. It is sometimes called "curvilinear," as forms become more complex, freer flowing, and curvaceous.

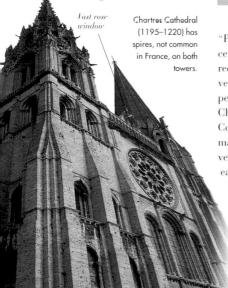

Vast rose window

Chartres Cathedral (1195–1220) has spires, not common in France, on both towers.

> ### NAMES ON THE WALL
>
> *Because of the uncertain nature of some architectural experimentation, many masons were paid handsome retainers to maintain their buildings. Some poor unfortunates found that they would never attend to anything else, giving a whole new meaning to "Gothic horror." The* **Countess Albereda of Bayeux** *beheaded her architect so that there could never be another castle built to match hers. In Germany, a knight moved by his faith to help build a cathedral was battered to death with hammers by hard-nosed regulars and thrown into the Rhine.*

In the last phase, late Gothic or "Perpendicular" (roughly fifteenth century), the tracery reverts to more rectilinear patterns, including multiple vertical divisions. The Perpendicular is peculiar to England. The Henry VII Chapel at Westminster (1503) and King's College Cambridge (1446) are the most magnificent examples. The plans are very simple—rectangular with apsidal east ends. But the spaces are dramatic—immensely tall and flooded with light through delicate tracery. In both, the spectacularly intricate vaulting owes more to decorative intention than structural logic.

1403 The City of Venice imposes quarantine on newcomers in an attempt to prevent recurrence of the Black Death that had ravaged Europe.

1414 The Florentine Medici family become the official bankers to the papacy.

1418 Henry V of England captures Rouen, the capital of Normandy.

1420~1550

Into the Light

Renaissance

Architecture gets into books.

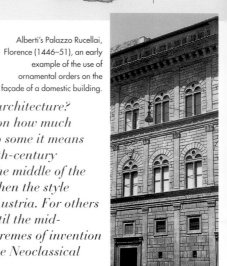

Alberti's Palazzo Rucellai, Florence (1446–51), an early example of the use of ornamental orders on the façade of a domestic building.

What is Renaissance architecture? The answer depends on how much of a purist you are. To some it means buildings from fifteenth-century Florence right up to the middle of the eighteenth century, when the style reached France and Austria. For others it describes only the period up until the mid-sixteenth century, after which extremes of invention in Baroque illusion or conservative Neoclassical revivalism take over.

Common to all is the starting point: the break with the feudal medieval past and a renewed interest in ancient Rome. Early exponents made careful studies of ancient remains in order to create faithful reproductions. Their drawings, printed for the first time, became "design guides" to the Classical orders. The work of those who subverted these rules or strayed too far from the correct uses of the orders was labeled with derogatory terms such as Mannerist, Baroque, and Rococo. Nowadays, such labels are often used descriptively without any sense of deprecation.

Orders is Orders

The Orders of Architecture relate to the columns you've seen propping up a building somewhere between the bank and city hall, or in some Hollywood epic. These uprights all have a base, a shaft, and a capital (the top bit), all in proportion, and ranging from the dull to the frankly florid. In order, then: Doric (Greek or Roman, sir? Greek? Without a base, then); Ionic, with a base and a scroll capital; and Corinthian, with a base and a capital showing off some restrained scroll-work, garnished with a little acanthus salad. Now repeat.

FROM ARTISAN TO PROFESSIONAL

In the past, architects were craftsmen closely linked to the construction process, and often directly involved in building. But when the cultural domination of the Church and patronage from prosperous families gave way to a new atmosphere of interest in the arts, the design of a building was seen as distinct from its construction. Architects had new creative status. This intellectual respectability was part of a wider movement with the creation of the first Italian academies in the second half of the sixteenth century.

1431 In France, Joan of Arc is burned at the stake for witchcraft.

1446 In Italy the Renaissance style Brunelleschi founded is taking off; in England the building of the Gothic King's College Chapel begins.

1506 Pope Julius II lays the foundation stone for St. Peter's Basilica in the Vatican, Rome.

NAMES ON THE WALL

When interest was reawakened in Roman construction, architecture was "extinct," according to the sixteenth-century art historian **Vasari,** *who linked Gothic with barbarism. Rome held everyone in thrall.* **Brunelleschi** *himself "stood like one amazed, and seemed to have lost his wits" when first he beheld it. Others sought any opportunity to visit and sketch.* **Giovan-Maria Falconetto** *set off on the 300-mile journey from Verona to Rome on the pretext of settling an argument about a cornice.*

PRINTING

The invention of printing resulted in the publication of the first architectural theories or treatises. Alberti's *De Re Aedificatoria* (1485) laid down a set of design rules based on the writings of

Vitruvius from the first century B.C. *SERLIO'S* (1475–1554) *L'architettura* (1537–51) was a reference manual for architects and builders. Palladio's theoretical writings, illustrated with examples of his own works as well as those of antiquity, were enormously influential. They continued to be a respected source well into the eighteenth century. The only work using medieval as well as ancient examples was Scamozzi's *L'idea dell'Architettura universale* (1615).

Putting Things into Perspective

Leon Battista Alberti (c.1404–72) is a contender for the title of Renaissance Man. His architecture works on the "quality, not quantity" theory (six designed, three built), but treat him gently: he's a major theorist, setting the tone for centuries of building with his *De Re Aedificatoria*, the first coherent publication on the use of the Classical orders. When talking of harmonic proportions, or architectural perspective, or the inspired Renaissance use of Roman building styles, drop Alberti's name. Pure gold dust.

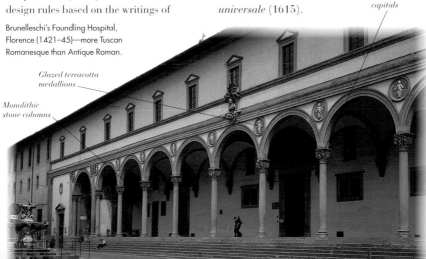

Brunelleschi's Foundling Hospital, Florence (1421–45)—more Tuscan Romanesque than Antique Roman.

Corinthian capitals

Glazed terracotta medallions

Monolithic stone columns

1450 Florence forms an alliance with Milan and Naples, ensuring peace and the flourishing of the arts in the three states. About the same time Alberti invents a device for measuring wind speed.

1450 Revision of the calendar commissioned by Julius Caesar, by now inaccurate, is begun. It will be 1582 when it is finally completed and everyone knows what day it is.

1452 Alberti writes his treatise on architecture in which he applies Pythagorean proportions of math and music to the 3D world.

1420~1500

There Is Nothing Like a Dome
Brunelleschi and Alberti

The octagonal, ribbed dome by Brunelleschi surmounting Florence Cathedral (1420–34).

Power and influence ruled supreme in early Renaissance Italy. Gone were the established hereditary aristocracy. In came the now-famous Italian families of merchants, Medici in Florence, Visconti and Sforza in Milan. With their new wealth came a new trend— patronage. It became fashionable to give money to the arts and artists and to build great palaces and churches. The quality of building and the flourishing of painting and sculpture in this period is attributed to the patronage of this new class.

It was the time for intellectual and artistic discovery and development: intellectuals were engaged in the search for order and meaning; painters discovered the rules of perspective; sculptors revealed the structures of human anatomy; and architects defined new rules of proportion, geometry, and symmetry. Innovative and dramatic achievements resulted.

BRUNELLESCHI

Filippo BRUNELLESCHI (1377–1446) started his career as a goldsmith and sculptor and went on to build the first of the great Renaissance domes to complete the church of Santa Maria del Fiore (1436) in Florence. He proposed to build an octagonal dome over the crossing without using temporary support. He did it, to universal admiration, by constructing a self-supporting hemispherical dome as formwork, which remained in position inside the octagonal dome.

In addition to experimenting with innovative structural techniques, he also pushed the limits of accepted knowledge in his use of geometry. The old sacristy (1428) in the church of San Lorenzo is one

1454–57 Uccello paints his battle paintings for the Palazzo Medici. He shows space, perspective, and three-dimensionality in a new way.

1458 The Turks sack the Acropolis in Athens.

1472 Ivan the Great makes himself Tsar of Russia and marries the niece of the last Byzantine emperor, aiming to make Moscow the new Constantinople.

such masterpiece. The design is evolved from the overlaying of two spheres of different diameters, one contained within and one penetrating the exterior of a perfect cube. The dramatic spatial effect is heightened by the stark contrast between the white plaster surfaces of the walls and the gray stonework. He was inspired by the twelfth-century Tuscan Romanesque.

ALBERTI

While Brunelleschi based his work on Romanesque and medieval sources, *Leon Battista ALBERTI* (1404–72), a writer and academic, as well as an architect, drew inspiration from ancient Rome for his buildings. His façade of Santa Maria Novella, Florence (1456), with its scrolls masking the existing aisle roof, became a much-copied pattern. At the Palazzo Rucellai (1451), a simple three-story form, he applied three levels of Classical orders to decorate the façade in imitation of the Colosseum in Rome. In his last work, the Church of St. Andrew in Mantua (1472), he employed a Roman monumental arch to design a striking façade that barely concealed the building behind it.

Everybody Must get Domed
From Rome's Pantheon to the Millennium in London's Greenwich, domes have been big business. They are beasts to build. Permanent formwork, conical timber frames, and encircling chains have been used in the most elaborate constructions. The outside dome, whether parachute, pumpkin, umbrella, or even onion, is rarely the same shape as the inside. The space between the inner and outer dome is often where the access stairs wind up to the lantern.

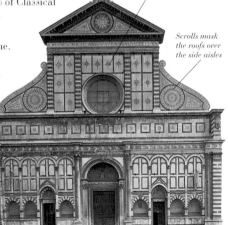
Polychromatic surface

Scrolls mask the roofs over the side aisles

Alberti's façade of Santa Maria Novella, Florence (1456), is "separate" from the building behind.

1452 Leonardo da Vinci, the Renaissance Man par excellence, is born.

1453-56 Athens is sacked. Greek scholars flee to Italian cities with nothing but their scholarship, which they impart to the Italians, and the Renaissance begins.

1477 Botticelli paints the perennial favorite *Primavera*, and the painter Titian is born.

1500~1530
Perfect Harmony
Bramante and Peruzzi

Harmony, simplicity, and repose characterized the High Renaissance period in Rome. What better location for a style based on antiquity than a city full of antiquities. In addition, the city was home to a wealthy papacy keen to reassert itself in the face of competition from the Protestant movement and new capitalism. Majestic building projects were an obvious means of showing who was top dog.

Bramante's Tempietto in the tranquil courtyard of San Pietro in Montorio, Rome (1502-1?) is a diminutive circular temple. The interior only 15 feet/4.5meters in diameter.

Rags-to-riches *Donato* BRAMANTE (1444–1514) was the main agent in recreating historically correct Roman buildings. From a poor background, Bramante had an innate talent that led him to be described by Palladio as "the first who brought good and beautiful architecture to light." His Tempietto

Raphael. Mister Perfect.

As a painter, this north Italian boy set benchmarks no one could beat for years, and condemned us all to Mannerism. His paintings, like *The Betrothal of the Virgin* (1504, Milan) and the frescoes of the Stanze (from 1508)—the rooms in the Vatican he decorated for Pope Julius II—are among his best works. But architecture was in Raphael's blood, though little of his work survives. His interest was probably inspired by his appointment as Supervisor of Roman Antiquities (1515), and by the antiquities around him. It didn't last. In demand everywhere, Raphael just couldn't cope with the Renaissance equivalent of executive stress. What a waste.

di San Pietro in Montorio (1502) is considered to be the perfect example of High Renaissance, extending the simple, austere aesthetic that faithfully follows the rules set down by Alberti. The central volume is enclosed by a Doric colonnade and entablature faithful to Roman principles, crowned with a (more Christian) drum and semicircular dome. The walls are decorated simply with niches and pilasters.

His big break came with the election of Pope Julius II, who asked him to prepare designs for the rebuilding of St. Peter's and the Vatican. Bramante proposed a centralized (Greek cross) plan, a symbol of perfection, with a dome the size of the Pantheon's and four smaller domes surrounding it—a symmetrical mass designed to stand in the center of a vast piazza. But in 1513, Pope Julius died and everything stopped.

1480–90 Navigators, including the Italian Cristoforo Columbo, explore the world, visiting many places previously known only to those living there.

1537 Andreas Vesalius becomes Professor of Anatomy at Padua and human dissection is put on the syllabus.

1543 Copernicus's *De Revolutionibus Orbium Caelestium* published, proposing the Sun as the center of the Cosmos.

Too Many Cooks?

The architects involved in the building and decor of St. Peter's and the Vatican read like the Renaissance Hall of Fame. Bramante, Michelangelo, Raphael, and Bernini were only four of the whiz kids involved. Bramante's plan for St. Peter's was the first, vast in concept and revolutionary for its time: an enormous square hall, with chapels symmetrically placed around it, and a dome stuck on top, resting on gigantic arches. Then a problem arises—the pope dies. Funds dry up, and it all changes. In 1514 Raphael takes over, and goes for a basilica instead. In 1520 Raphael dies. Peruzzi takes over, followed by Sargallo in 1539. Most of the work they do to alter Bramante's original will later be demolished.

PERUZZI

Twenty years later and all the Classical rules are being ignored. Repose is out; dynamic and theatrical effect is in. This "Mannerist" trend is ushered in by *Baldassare PERUZZI* (1481–1536), whose finest work is the Villa Farnesina (1511). The plan includes a loggia in the center of the garden elevation and principal rooms located on the ground floor rather than the first floor. Peruzzi's other masterpiece is the Palazzo Massimo alle Colonne (1532–36), where Mannerist unorthodoxy is very obvious. Contrary to all the rules, the building is asymmetrical and follows the curve of the road. The façade similarly flouts convention. In contrast to a heavily rusticated base with Ionic columns, the upper levels are smooth, with minimal surface articulation.

NAMES ON THE WALL

There seems to be a rule that authoritative commentators on architectural history must have names beginning with V. We have already encountered **Vitruvius**. *Now we meet* **Vignola** *and* **Vasari**. *Giorgio* **Vasari's** *Lives of the Artists reflects the true diversity of Renaissance practitioners whose skills encompassed architecture, mathematics, painting, sculpture, and science.* **Giacomo Barozzi da Vignola** *produced* Regole delle cinque ordine, *a "how-to" book that was hugely popular.*

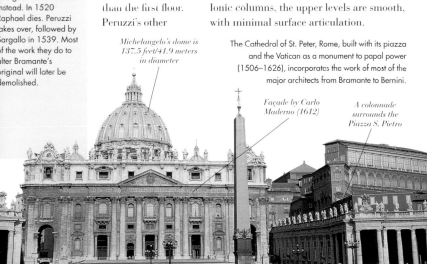

Michelangelo's dome is 137.5 feet/41.9 meters in diameter

The Cathedral of St. Peter, Rome, built with its piazza and the Vatican as a monument to papal power (1506–1626), incorporates the work of most of the major architects from Bramante to Bernini.

Façade by Carlo Maderno (1612)

A colonnade surrounds the Piazza S. Pietro

1475 In Bruges, William Caxton (c. 1422–91) prints the first book in the English language: *Recuyell of the Historyes of Troye*.

1450–1667 St. Peter's in Rome rebuilt. Rossellini, Bramante, Raphael, da Sangallo, Michelangelo, della Porta, Fontana, Maderno, and Bernini all lend a hand and the result is a combination of Renaissance, Mannerist, and Baroque.

1495 Syphilis spreads from Naples. French sailors are held to be blame.

1530~1570

Michelangelo
Yes, That Michelangelo

The Vitruvian rules, followed with such rigor and meticulous care by Bramante, were rejected by the inspired and imaginative MICHELANGELO (1475–1564)— poet, painter, sculptor, and great architect. Harmony and repose, the key to the style of ancient civilizations, were rejected as he reinvented all the rules of composition in pursuit of tension, drama, and an assault on all the senses, not just the eyes.

Big Mike

Michelangelo Buonarre beggars description. Everything about this revolutionary, non-Albertian artist-archite was and is larger tha life. But the vain workaholic painter we know best for his sculpture and the Sistine ceiling was a truly great architect. Michelangelo challenged and changed the nature o space in architecture, setting down his idea in model form, rather than on paper. This typically energetic output has been unjustly bypassed in popular mythology, partly because of the Sistine achievement, and perhaps because all his architectural work was incomplete at his death; it was finished, in good taste or bad, by others.

Despite his great architectural achievements, Michelangelo's name is primarily known for his frescoes on the ceiling of the Sistine Chapel in the Vatican (1508–12), depicting stories from Genesis.

The Medici family mausoleum in the sacristy of San Lorenzo, Florence (1521), is the earliest example of the revolutionary design by Michelangelo. Both the plan arrangement and the use of gray stone and white plaster are very similar to the old sacristy, but the composition of visual and decorative elements is wildly unconventional: huge cornices above the doors seem barely able to support vast tabernacles; the group of figures is 13 feet above the ground, drawing the eye upward; the columns are no longer underneath the entablature. The wall is no longer simply a flat surface to which decoration has been added—it has become a sculptural element.

c. 1550 The Renaissance flourishes. At the same time the Italians develop a taste for billiards.

1561 Completion of the onion-domed St. Basil's basilica in Moscow, built by Ivan the Terrible (1530–84) to celebrate his various victories.

1564 William Shakespeare, Christopher Marlowe, and Galileo are born; the Roman Church publishes an index of prohibited books.

WHEN IN ROME

In 1534 Michelangelo undertook his first commission in Rome—nothing less than to reorganize the Capitol. The design displays the same sculptural effects and unusual elements that characterized his work in Florence. The square is organized around a raised oval ground plane—the first time the oval is used—and the façades splay outward, distorting the perspective. In contrast to the controlled view in the rectilinear spaces of the Early Renaissance, the area is intended to be viewed from different angles, with different perspectives unfolding as the viewer moves around. The façades have a "giant order," with the columns ignoring the floor levels to unify the elevation—a common feature of Mannerist architecture.

Michelangelo reverted to Bramante's ideas when he was assigned to the

Brunelleschi's chapel of San Lorenzo contains the Medici family vault. Michelangelo's earliest architectural piece.

completion of St. Peter's in 1546. He demolished most of the additions of Raphael and Sangallo and continued with Bramante's original centralized plan and a smaller dome. Much of Michelangelo's work is obscured by alterations to the nave and the façade designed by *Carlo MADERNO* (1566-1629), which were completed in 1612.

NAMES ON THE WALL

Giulio Romano *(1492–1546), a painter and architect, took an approach to Mannerism that has been called expressionist, intended to involve the visitor in the sensuous experience of the building. His Palazzo del Te in Mantua (1526–31) is a single-story building with a courtyard. The façades are revolutionary; Serlian windows on a flat surface on one side contrast with solid and heavy rustications on the other. The heavy Tuscan order is used. The interiors feature frescoes of erotic subjects that are difficult to ignore.*

Laurentian Library

The cloister of San Lorenzo in Florence is the location of the famous Laurentian Library vestibule (1526), the tall, square space filled with a cascade of three staircases. Again there are a whole series of unorthodox features: consoles that support nothing, aedicules with pilasters tapering at the bottom, and columns paired in recesses, rather like statues in niches. The curious and unexpected grabs our attention. There is no figurative sculpture; the architecture itself becomes plastic, nonfigurative, abstract sculpture instead.

1531 The comet known as "the Great Comet" causes consternation; one of six to terrify the world (the new astronomers excepted) in the 1530s.

c. 1550–72 The Benedictine monastery at Tivoli is rebuilt as the lavish Villa d'Este with fountains, ornamental lake, cascades, water jets, water organ, grottoes, et al.

1566–78 Vignola completes the Villa Lante at Bagnaia (near Viterbo). One of the features of gardens is a series of water-cooled dining tables.

1510~1590

Mind Your Mannerism
Vignola

Following in the footsteps of someone as great as Michelangelo might seem the worst of jobs for anyone, but Giacomo BAROZZI DA VIGNOLA (1507–73) proved himself equal to the challenge. He succeeded Michelangelo at St. Peter's and as Rome's leading architect. He studied painting and architecture in Bologna before moving to Rome, where his numerous churches and exceptionally beautiful villas have been enormously influential.

The Villa Giulia (1551–55), built for Pope Julius III, is an impressive spatial composition and an important conceptual development. While Michelangelo sculpted walls, Vignola sculpted volume and space. Vignola's walls function both as the boundary enclosing inner space, and as an outside space, and the line between the interior and the exterior is blurred. Immediately beyond the façade, a relatively austere symmetrical rectangular form, is an open semicircular courtyard. The vista is framed on both sides and

Villa Giulia is dominated by a massive rusticated portal. The large voussoirs (stones forming the arch) overlap the entablature above.

That Cool, Clear Water

Characteristically the Romans developed and provided the means to deliver water across rough terrain to your door … well, almost. Their aqueducts were arched masonry structures in stone or brick, sometimes of a massive size, supporting a stone channel in which the wet stuff flowed. Spectacular examples are the Pont du Gard (1st century B.C.) near Nîmes, France, and a 2nd century A.D. aqueduct at Segovia, Spain, which still does the business for the locals. It didn't end there: English engineers also constructed aqueducts for barge transportation during the great canal era of the eighteenth century.

1577 The Church of the Redentore is commissioned from Palladio to celebrate the end of a bad plague in Venice.

1573 English architect Inigo Jones and Italian painter Michelangelo da Caravaggio born.

1590–1600 The theater, with plays by Shakespeare, Jonson, and Marlowe, is flourishing in London.

* side nave with nnel vault of*

Decorative scrolls mask aisle roofs

The Gesù, Rome, by Vignola (begun 1568) has a façade designed by Giacomo della Porta.

The loggia in the courtyard of the Villa Giulia provides shade from the Roman sun.

closed by a semitransparent loggia that divides the courtyard in two. Concealed steps lead down to a lower level, and the dark secrets of the watery nymphaneum beneath. The unexpected formal arrangements—juxtaposition of straight and curved walls, the hidden spaces suddenly revealed—are all part of the unsettling effect of the succession of spaces.

Vignola's Gesù (1568), built for the Society of Jesus, symbolized the reestablishment of Catholicism, and both its plan and elevation were much copied. It is a combination of Renaissance planning (a centralized east end with a domed crossing) and a Latin cross plan with an extended nave. In place of side aisles there are chapels opening directly off the central nave. The façade is a basilican form with decorative scrolls reminiscent of Alberti's Santa Maria Novella.

Giorgio VASARI (1511–74), a painter and great fan of Michelangelo, was involved with Vignola and Ammanati on the Villa Giulia. His Uffizi (1560) in Florence is based on Michelangelo's Laurentian Library.

NAMES ON THE WALL

Giacomo della Porta *(1533–1602), best known for the fantastic Villa Aldobrandini in Frascati (1598–1603), followed Vignola as architect at the Gesù, where he designed the façade (1571–84). He also followed Michelangelo at St. Peter's (1573–74) and completed the dome (1588–90) and the garden façades.* **Carlo Maderno's** *task when he was appointed to St. Peter's in 1603 was to add the by now compulsory nave and a new façade. His other important works are Santa Susanna and San Andrea della Vallee.*

1508 Michelangelo begins his monumental work, painting the Sistine Chapel ceiling.

1511 The text of Vitruvius's ancient treatise *De Architectura*, dedicated to Augustus and in circulation again since 1414, is now published (in Latin and later in Italian, French, Spanish).

1518 "Cigaritos"— small cigars from the New World—are being imported into Europe by Spanish traders.

1540~1580
Palladio
Italian High Renaissance

Unique as the only architect to have an idiom, Palladianism, named after him, Andrea PALLADIO (1508–80) has to be one of the best known of all architects. His work represents an architecture logical in approach and resulting in a calm serenity and a practical functionality. "Usefulness," "durability," and "beauty" are the three essentials Palladio advocated, to be achieved through the careful application of the rules of composition derived from ancient civilization and based on the laws of nature: symmetry and harmony.

Palladio has an enormous number of buildings of all types to his credit, as well as extensive writings, including *I quattro libri dell'Architettura* (1570), which became the standard Neoclassical reference for centuries afterward. His first project, won in competition in 1549, was for the remodeling of the Basilica of Vicenza. He enclosed the existing building within a two-storied, colonnaded screen wall using the Serlian windows (renamed Palladian) said to be copied from the Roman baths of Diocletian. The Palazzo Thiene (1542) has pilasters paired in the corner bays and is heavily rusticated. Both the Palazzo Chiercati (1550), with its two-story portico, and Palazzo Valmarana (1565), with its giant composite pilasters and superimposed Corinthian columns, include a variety of stucco decoration.

Andrea Palladio

What a boy. No frills, no sidelines. Just a builder, pure and simple. He learned well from Michelangelo, Raphael, Bernini, and others, and used his avid interest in archeology in his designs, mostly for the better. But while his Italian creations are legendary, Palladio's influence elsewhere, in Britain especially, could be and was revolutionary. It actually changed the landscape. If Inigo Jones (1573–1652) hadn't been such a slavish admirer, and if the great Kunstführer Lord Burlington (1694–1753) hadn't followed suit, the British country house tradition (and with it Britain's National Trust) might never have existed. Think about it.

The church of San Giorgio Maggiore in Venice sto reflected in the Lagoon. The faç of Palladio's church was comple by Scamozzi in 1602–

Domed crossing

Nave has g order and t front pedim

1530 The Venetian Giovanni Spinetti invents the spinet, to be played in the gracious new Italian villas.

c. 1550 Gabriele Fallopio of Padua University, discoverer of Fallopian tubes, invents the condom, to be used as a means of preventing the spread of infection.

1565 The first description of the pencil is given by the Swiss Conrad Gesner. Pencil drawing becomes widespread.

THE VILLAS

While the palazzos show a Mannerist tendency and a variety of design ideas, the numerous villas Palladio designed conform to a standard pattern that was both functional and flexible. Most, such as Villa Poiana, Poiana Maggiore (1549), Villa Pisani, Bagnolo (1544), and Saraceno, Firale di Agugliaro (1545), are based around a centralized square plan, have a rectangular *salone*, and temple front porticoes. Other spaces, such as stables, granaries, or barns, are then arranged symmetrically as variations on the basic theme. One of the more unusual, the Villa Rotonda, near Vicenza, is a variant that uses a circular domed *salone* and has a portico on all four façades overlooking the surrounding countryside.

NAMES ON THE WALL

Readers needing an aide mémoire *might like to know that* **Palladio's** *real family name was* **Gondola**. *Despite demonstrating a detailed knowledge of Roman antiquities in his books, he made free with Mannerist detail and misplaced temple-front porticoes in his own work! The tide of publications gave rise to fears that originality would be stultified by obeisance to the past. Nevertheless, faced with the choice of one architectural tome to take to a desert island,* **Martin Briggs** *thought it would be* **Vasari's** *Lives, not* **Palladio's** *Orders.*

Palladio's churches are less well known but none the less beautiful and accomplished works. San Giorgio Maggiore, Venice (1565), is a Benedictine church with a Latin cross plan, side aisles, and a retrochoir. The simple, austere finishes of the interior are lit by Palladian windows high in the nave. The later Redentore, Venice (1577), is simpler in plan, with a single nave and side chapels and a monks' choir behind a screen. The façade, composed with both giant and small orders, accentuates the complex three-dimensional composition of dome, turrets, and buttresses.

School's Out

The growth of the academy as a teaching institution was a slow one, and architects weren't recognized as a breed apart: they were lumped in with the painters and sculptors. The breakthrough came in France, in 1671, where special training for architectural wannabes was provided at the newly formed academy. It was a drop in the ocean. Architectural instruction tended to stay informal, largely because the printed sources were few. Throughout Europe, the eighteenth-century Enlightenment moved matters forward, and as academies began to appear, professional training followed suit.

The Villa Rotonda, Vicenza (1552), has a portico on each of the four façades.

1517 The portrait of Pope Leo X by Raphael shows the pontiff wearing spectacles. Glass manufacture (based in Venice and Nuremberg) now makes many more readers use eyeglasses.

1528 In Germany, despite Renaissance influences, Gothic art is going strong. Grünewald completes the Isenheim altarpiece at Colmar.

1550 Viols, recorders, and the lute are essential instruments in court and stately home.

1500~1600

Châteaux and Palais

French Renaissance

The Palais de Fontainebleau (1528–40), Seine-et-Marne, built for François I, gains much of its effect from the reflection in one of its lakes.

A particularly French version of Italian Renaissance architecture was established during the sixteenth century with the building of châteaux, many in the Loire Valley, which was initially promoted as the location of François I and his court. The Château du Bury (1511–24, destroyed) was the model. Plans are generally square, with circular towers (pavilions) at the corners crowned with conical roofs. The buildings are often only one room deep, with the principal rooms situated between the courtyard and the garden, and service spaces adjacent to stableyards or ancillary courtyards. There is a tendency for façades to be ornate and crowded with sculpture and carvings, rather than monumental.

The Château de Chambord (1519–47) is the most spectacular, with all the characteristics of a fairy-tale castle. A square building with four round pavilions at the corners sits inside a rectangular four-towered *enceinte* surrounded by a moat—a simple medieval model. The interior is completely symmetrical. It has two axial, rectangular vaulted halls making a cross in plan, with a fantastic double-helix staircase behind openwork balustrading placed centrally at the intersection. No encounter is possible on the staircase; climbers circle each other, ascending and descending. In the corner on each floor are

NAMES ON THE WALL

France's invasion of Italy in 1494 brought Renaissance architecture to the attention of the French court in a way that no simple lecture tour could. Colonies of Italian artists resided at Amboise, Tours, and Blois. Meanwhile, "master mason" types of the medieval period like **Gilles Le Breton** *continued to operate, and increasingly established craft dynasties. Responsibility for masterpieces such as the Loire châteaux is hotly contested, and one theory holds that the* **King (François I)** *dunnit.*

1550 Coal begins to replace wood as an industrial fuel. Mines open at Liège and Newcastle. Weapons of war are the main industrial product.

1600 By this year, William Shakespeare has written twenty plays, including *As You Like It*, and *A Midsummer Night's Dream*.

c. 1610 The first appearance of the violin. Louis XIII of France has a group known as the Vingt-quatre Violins du Roi. Baroque music gets going.

Gridiron to Gridlock

Town planning really began in the ancient world with the simple introduction of the rectilinear grid for streets. In France, King Henri IV (1553–1610) was more interested in town planning than in building châteaux. Inspired by Sixtus V's plan for Rome, he introduced radial planning with public squares and "places" at the street intersections. The Place des Vosges (originally Place Royale), which has a colonnaded street level, was the first such public space, surrounded by houses. Centuries later, Baron Haussman (1809–91) reorganized the streets of Paris, based on the same ideas. Circular boulevards and radiating avenues were intended to create monumental vistas, as well as control the inhabitants.

identical *logis* comprising salon, bed chamber, and *cabinet*. Elaborate lanterns light the staircases and crowds of dormers and tall chimneys punctuate the roof, which can be explored via a balustraded terrace below the eaves.

BLOIS AND CHENONCEAU

At the earlier Château de Blois (1515–24), François I added a wing to the existing medieval castle. The wing is more Italian, with *loggias* based on Bramante's work at the Vatican.

The Château de Chenonceau (1515–23) has the square block, four pavilions, and steeply pitched roofs. The romantic bridge across the Cher (1556–59) was added later by *Philibert DE L'ORME* (1510–70) for Diane de Poitiers, the mistress of Henri II.

The château at Azay-le-Rideau (1519–27), Indre-et-Loire, was built for a wealthy bourgeois family on the banks of the Indre River.

THE LOUVRE AND FONTAINEBLEAU

François I was also responsible for starting rebuilding work at the Louvre, Paris, which was to continue for several centuries. *Pierre LESCOT* (1500–78) made an important contribution to French Classicism with his design for the Cour Carré (1546–51), and Philibert de l'Orme began designs to connect the Louvre to the Palais des Tuileries. *Jean DU CERCEAU* (c. 1590–c. 1649) is the other important architect, remembered for his ostentatious horseshoe-shaped staircase at the Palais de Fontainebleau, the largest château of them all.

Philibert de l'Orme had considerable influence through his writings, *Nouvelles Inventions* (1561) and *Architecture* (1567) —a practical work explaining how to construct a house. Du Cerceau was equally influential through his publication *Les plus excellents bâtiments de France* (1576–79).

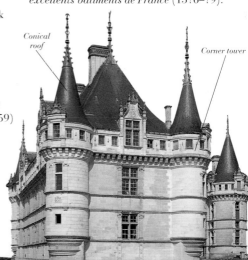

Conical roof

Corner tower

1529 Cardinal Wolsey falls from grace and Henry VIII takes over his palace at Hampton Court. Wolsey should have known better than to outbuild the king.

1530 England leaves Rome and the Reformation follows. Dissolution of the monasteries means the poor have no one to care for them, but the better-off have stone to build with.

1530 The potato is introduced to Europe from South America.

1520~1630

Gloriana
Tudor and Elizabethan England

Unlike the grandeur and austerity of Italian and French Renaissance architectures, that of Tudor England was still medieval in spirit, with informal planning and Gothic craftsmanship. But when the wealthy aristocrats and the rich merchant bourgeoisie all began to aspire to having a place in the country, architects heeded the call, and the Renaissance-influenced Elizabethan mansion started to appear.

SPOT THE STYLE

• Strapwork—interlaced patterns as if in leather or metal, woven together

• Plans and façades are symmetrical, learned from the Renaissance buildings in Europe

• Decoration is Dutch, with gables and strapwork

• Big windows with stone mullions and transoms

Timber Shortages

Town houses were still generally timber-framed, often with "jettied" construction (the first floor projects beyond the ground floor). Little Moreton Hall, in Cheshire (1559), and Pitchford, in Shropshire (1560), are the best-preserved examples of "black and white" Elizabethan houses. By the end of the sixteenth century, timber shortages and consequent price rises led to the development of alternatives. The more economical box frame with fewer timbers, or misshapen timbers that previously would have been rejected, were used with plastering to conceal the shortcomings.

The grandest Tudor house is Hampton Court Palace (1520), begun by Cardinal Wolsey. Henry VIII then claimed it for himself because it was bigger and better than his old timber-framed palace in Surrey, Nonsuch. Built in brick, the house is distinctively English, with its elaborate chimneys, stone-mullioned windows, castellations, and octagonal towers—all elements that were used throughout the sixteenth century. The great hall has a fine hammer-beam roof and oriel window.

THE AGE OF ELIZABETH

During Elizabeth's reign, a more geometric and symmetrical Renaissance style of planning developed. Façades followed suit, but differed radically from the Italian and French style with the use of Dutch gables and strapwork, and in continuing the Perpendicular passion for very large windows with masonry mullions and transoms. The principal room was the two-story great hall, often containing the main

1550–87 Burghley House is built in Cambridgeshire for William Cecil, Elizabeth I's chief adviser. Meanwhile, instead of building her own palaces Elizabeth I sleeps in other people's.

1560s England is gripped by a building boom as the middle classes emerge. E-shaped houses become popular.

c. 1584–89 Sir Walter Raleigh attempts to colonize part of North America and names Virginia after the Virgin Queen.

stair. The corridor at first-floor level connecting the rooms widened and developed into the long gallery, a space intended for the display of paintings.

Longleat, in Wiltshire (1567), designed by *Robert SMYTHSON* (1535–1614), is the earliest example of the style. The plan, arranged around two inner courtyards, has rigorously symmetrical façades, continuous entablatures, and pilastered projecting bays. Wollaton Hall, in Nottingham (1580), also by Smythson, is castlelike, with turrets around a central block containing the symmetrically planned main hall and square towers at each corner. The exterior has strapwork on Dutch gables and superimposed flat pilasters, paired in various different ways, between continuous entablatures at each floor level.

Little Moreton Hall, Cheshire (1550–59), a typical Tudor courtier's home, manages to house a long gallery. Timber framing is put to ornamental use (some call this early Renaissance).

Burghley House (1552–87), in Cambridgeshire, has the archetypal Tudor "look," with corner towers and square turrets, while Hardwick Hall, in Derbyshire (1590), has the façade with the most windows, giving rise to the wry comment "Hardwick Hall, more glass than wall."

The style continued in similar fashion into the reign of *JAMES I* (1603–25). Of note are Audley End, in Essex (1603), which has rather picturesque turrets above an otherwise very simple, symmetrical façade, and Hatfield House, in Hertfordshire (1607), where the south façade has an arcade on the ground floor below the long gallery.

Dissolution and other Protestant vices

Henry VIII's lousy love life (the pope wouldn't grant him a divorce from Catherine of Aragon) had one major result, in that he came down in favor of the Lutheran Reformation in all its austerity. The logical result was that all Roman associations were out, and so the monastic foundations had to go. In architectural terms the period known as the Dissolution of the Monasteries was a collective act of unbridled vandalism on the part of a king who prided himself on his intellect and education. Did Henry have a moral point? Were the monasteries corrupt? By that time, very likely. But the architectural damage done was horrendous.

Entablature unites articulated bays

Longleat, in Wiltshire, built for Sir John Thynne by Robert Smythson in the 1570s, has the requisite long gallery, grand staircase, and terraced entrance.

1601 Inigo takes his first Italian holiday and comes back full of architectural ideas.

1605 In the year of the Gunpowder Plot, Inigo designs his first masque, an early form of pantomime. He introduces Baroque to the English stage.

1620 The London Virginia Company finances the Pilgrim Fathers' first trip to Massachusetts and can be held responsible for Thanksgiving turkey dinners.

1573~1652
The Welsh Wizard
Inigo Jones

Queen's House floor plan.

The severe Classicism of the Italian Renaissance was introduced to England in the early seventeenth century by Inigo JONES (1573–1652). In the context of the picturesque Tudor style then current, Jones's buildings were a dramatic contrast. Jones had visited Italy and met Scamozzi, who was responsible for completing much of Palladio's work; Jones became an ardent admirer. As Surveyor to the King's Works between 1615 and 1642, Jones had worked on several prominent buildings, and his stylistic approach became enormously influential as the basis of the eighteenth-century Palladian revival.

Jones's masterpiece, the Banqueting House, in London (1619–22), is clearly Palladian in inspiration. The plan is rectangular and the volume is a double cube including a gallery. The façade is divided into three; the center with protruding half columns and balconies, the two sides with flatter pilasters and panels. It has a rusticated base, first-floor windows with alternating segmental and triangular pediments, and top-floor windows with straight cornices. It is best described in Jones's words, "sollid proporsionable according to the rulles, masculine and unaffected."

The Banqueting House at Whitehall was the only building in Jones's plan for the new palace to be completed.

CUBES AND SQUARES

The Queen's House at Greenwich (1616–18) is a reinterpretation of a Palladian villa, complete with a loggia at first-floor level and curved symmetrical flights of steps up to the terrace. Again symmetry and proportion are paramount: the hall inside is a perfect cube.

1632 The painter Van Dyck comes to work in England at the court of Charles I and is soon joined by his disciple Peter Lely.

1649 Charles I of England is executed; England declares a commonwealth, which is set up under Oliver Cromwell.

1652 The society of Friends (Quakers) is founded in England.

Jones's Pupil

Roger Pratt (1620–85), a talented follower of Inigo Jones, was responsible for setting the trend for simple classical houses. Coleshill House, in Berkshire (c.1650, demolished 1952), was the finest, with a double square plan and tripartite elevations based on Palladio.

Jones was also responsible for the original design of London's first square, at Covent Garden, with a colonnaded street level and giant pilasters above. The only surviving piece is the church of St. Paul, with detail faithful to Vitruvius, a heavy Tuscan portico, and a simple rectangular plan. Appropriate for Protestant worship and to suit the economic constraints of his client, this structure was defined by Jones as "the handsomest barn in England."

NAMES ON THE WALL

Inigo Jones Senior was a Smithfield cloth worker who was fined for bad language and went bankrupt in 1589. Jones Junior first found renown as an originator of royal masques. On a second visit to Italy at age 40, he was still sketching the human figure more than architectural details. Given this late start, it is clear that many more buildings have been attributed to him than can possibly be his. It is likely that more credit should go to his assistants John Webb and Nicholas Stone.

The Queen's House, in Greenwich, is plain and well proportioned. The queen in question was Queen Anne, although it was completed for Henrietta Maria, wife of Charles I.

Ground-floor windows were dropped in 1770

Façade has three divisions

Open loggia with Ionic columns

1595 The Carracci found their painting academy and inspire a generation of artists to work in the Baroque manner, adding emotion and individuality to Classicism.

1637 Philosopher René Descartes (1596–1650) publishes his *Discourses on Method*. He thinks, therefore he is.

1646 The English Civil War ends with victory for Parliament and for the Puritans.

1620~1830

The Fabulous Baroque Boys
Baroque in Italy

The oval dome of Borromini's San Carlo alle Quattro Fontane, Rome.

"Irregular shapes and extravagant ornamentation" is the hopelessly inadequate definition often used to describe, in purely visual terms, an architecture that has to be experienced to be believed. The Baroque churches of Rome, built by popes competing to have more and more splendid places of worship to their names, were everything that the austere temples of the Reformation were not: opulent, rich, dramatic, and exciting. They represent the Catholic Church at its most powerful.

Baroque churches are filled with a sense of movement, full of sensual shapes and curvaceous, sinuous, and serpentine spaces. The clearly understandable static space of the perfect circle, and the processional space of the rectilinear nave, are replaced by oval plans and walls punctuated with niches and alcoves of all shapes and sizes. Façades change from convex to concave and back again, their pilasters crowded together, adding depth and shadow to the undulating surface. Columns are now into spiral twists, the known orders are distorted, and the pediments are broken, riotously curved, and tilted every which way. Spaces appear to have been carved from solid shapes.

THE RIVALS

Two architects stand out. One, *Francesco BORROMINI* (1599–1677), is the sensitive soul—a working man and a first-rate craftsman. The other, *Gianlorenzo BERNINI* (1598–1680), from a wealthy family, is self-assured, multitalented, and favored by wealthy patrons. Neither has much time for the other.

Borromini started his career as a stone cutter at St. Peter's, where he was eventually to become Bernini's assistant. Among his best works are two very small churches. The chapel of San Carlo alle Quattro Fontane (1638–46) is formed from the geometry of interlocking triangles, and has several oval side chapels that somehow seem to merge

1648 In France the first of the uprisings known as the Frondes takes place.

1660 The English monarchy is restored; the reign of Charles II opens the door to theater and theatricality.

1683 Dutch lens grinder Antonie van Leeuwenhoek sees tiny living beings through his microscope.

together magically to become the fluid oval form of the dome above. In San Ivo della Sapienza (1642–60), where the chapel is first seen at a distance across a courtyard, the dome becomes a spiraling ziggurat on the outside.

One of Bernini's earliest commissions was the baldacchino (1623–33) at the crossing under the dome at St. Peter's. With enormous twisted spiral columns, sumptuous decoration, and rich materials, it is somewhat grandiose. His most powerful sculptural work is the Coronaro Chapel in Santa Maria della Vittoria, where he uses light and false perspective, multicolored marble, and a theatrical setting to heighten the eroticism of the subject, the ecstasy of St. Theresa. In his *Fountain of the Rivers* (1648) in the Piazza Navona, one of the figures is covering his face—allegedly so that he doesn't have to see the façade of the church opposite, which was designed by Borromini.

NAMES ON THE WALL

The career of **Domenico Fontana** *(1543–1601) illustrates the importance of papal patronage and the unconventional modus operandi of some popes. Engaged in building a chapel for* **Cardinal Montalto** *and finding the cardinal's funds suspended,* **Fontana** *deployed 1,000 crowns of his own money to complete the task. Soon afterward,* **Montalto** *became* **Pope Sixtus V** *and Fontana's career trajectory was ensured. This same pope was guilty of ransacking Rome's architectural heritage, and ordered Fontana to convert the Colosseum into a wool factory.*

Dynamic sculpture

St. Peter's tomb

Twisted columns

The baldacchino, or tomb canopy, under Michelangelo's dome in St. Peter's, Rome, is an early work by Bernini.

1605 The Place Royale (now Place des Vosges) in Paris is completed but traffic circulation is already a growing problem.

1607 Claudio Monteverdi (1567–1643) writes the first real opera; *La Favola d'Orfeo.*

1610 Galileo discovers (with the aid of his adaptation of the new telescope) the moons of Jupiter and phases of Venus.

1600~1700

Baroque en France
Mansart, Le Vau

The Baroque in France comprises the same formal and decorative elements that are found in Italy— but a certain French coolness means that the extravagant drama is tempered with a degree of Classical restraint.

Le Vau's château at Vaux-le-Vicomte, built for Nicholas Fouquet, Surintendant des Finances.

Two figures stand out in this period. François MANSART (1598–1666) and Louis LE VAU (1612–70), contemporaries working under Louis XIV, were responsible for the most important buildings of the French Baroque.

Mansart's Maisons Lafitte (1642–48) has oval rooms and "mansard roofs," which were named after him. The church of Val-de-Grace, Paris (1645), has a façade in a restrained, earlier Renaissance style and a dome—a recently introduced feature in French buildings.

Le Vau had the peculiarly Baroque talent of combining architecture with sculpture, painting, and decorating to produce some of the most flamboyant works of the period. His masterpiece is the house at Vaux-le-Vicomte (1657–61), one of the most brilliant of all French châteaux. The house has a magnificent central domed salon on an oval plan, rich decoration by Lebrun (1619–90), and fabulous gardens laid out by *André LE NÔTRE* (1613–1700).

NAMES ON THE WALL

The Russian tsarina **Elizabeth Petrovna** *proved an enlightened architectural patron. The ladies of the French court were mad about architecture;* **Catherine de Medici** *and* **Diane de Poitiers** *(mistress of Henri II) vied for supremacy in this as in all things. Diane was more successful, as Catherine was afflicted with "building mania" and "very bad taste." It was the* **Marquise de Rambouillet,** *however, who made the enlightened suggestion that "cabinets de toilettes, salles des bains, and the like, ought to be near bedrooms instead of at the other end of the garden."*

Early 17th-c. Music is for dancing as well as listening to: rooms need to provide space for up to 40 musicians as well as the dancers.

1678 John Bunyan's novel *Pilgrim's Progress* is published. It is an allegory of man's journey through life.

1683 The Ottoman Turks besiege Vienna but are repelled. They leave coffee beans behind and the Viennese coffee house is born.

Jules HARDOUIN-MANSART (1646–1708, the great-nephew of François) was appointed royal architect in 1675 and continued Le Vau's work at the palace of Versailles in the 1670s, including the magnificent Galerie des Glaces. The famous gardens at Versailles, laid out by Le Nôtre, allow long vistas as an extension of the enfilade, the linear arrangement of the interior spaces within the palace. This kind of axial planning with focal points, radiating vistas, and monumental effects is typical of urban design at the time. Hardouin-Mansart created the Parisian *places* Vendôme and Victoires. The chapel of Les Invalides (1680–91) has an oval chancel and a dramatic dome with one of the most extreme of Baroque illusionistic effects. Paintings on the outer dome become visible through an opening in the inner dome and are lit naturally by concealed windows.

Les Pautres

Antoine Le Pautre (1621–81) is another remarkably inventive architect of seventeenth-century France. His Hôtel de Beauvais, Paris (1652–55), is a truly ingenious piece of planning on a complicated urban site, jammed in between other buildings. He uses a whole variety of different shapes and configurations to great effect. He is also known for his book *Desseins de plusieurs palais* (1652), which features engraved designs for huge and extravagantly Baroque country houses. Le Pautre's nephew Pierre (c.1643–1716) was influential in developing the Rococo style of decoration and was the leading decorator at Versailles under Hardouin-Mansart, responsible for the palace's chapel.

Russia

The westernization of Russian architecture is usually associated with the "Moscow" or "Naryskin" Baroque of the 1680s and 90s: still largely medieval but with some Classical symmetry and application of the Classical orders. During the reign of Peter the Great (1682–1725), and with the founding of St. Petersburg (1703), western influences increased. Bartolomeo Rastrelli (1700–71), Empress Elizabeth's architect, was inspired by Versailles but also retained the Russian polychromatic decorations.

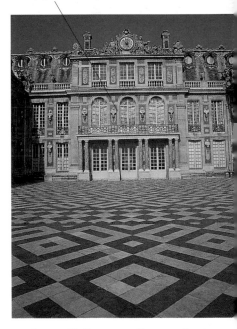

Symmetrical façade

Versailles, remodeled for Louis XIV, is the best-known work of the French Baroque. The Versailles style was created by Le Vau, although later work by Hardouin-Mansart obscured much of the original vision.

1717 In France the painter Watteau introduces the genre of painting known as the *fête galante.* Lightness, elegance, and delight rule the day.

1730s In England gin-drinking (an idea fostered by the Dutch) accounts for one in seven adult deaths. This state of affairs lasts until a tax is imposed on gin in 1751.

1735 Charles Marie de la Condamine discovers rubber while in South America measuring the curvature of the earth.

1650~1790
Gay but not Gaudy
Rococo

Rococo is often used to describe buildings of the last phase of the Baroque, mainly in Austria and southern Germany, where Protestantism was slow to take up such an ostentatious style. Rococo describes a kind of decoration: light, white, and asymmetrical, often with rustic scenes, naturalistic curves, and shell-like forms. It originated in France with rocaille, *the term for the rocklike encrustations used for grottoes and on fountains. There is also a spatial complexity usually attributed to the influence of the work of the Italian Guarino GUARINI (1624–83). Guarini's work, with a complex use of undulating concave and convex forms, is a synthesis of the geometries of Borromini and the illusionistic effects of Bernini, together with a rich ornamentation of his own.*

The Karlskirche in Vienna has a variety of borrowed Roman elements, expressively used.

Oriental roof-line

Johann Bernhard FISCHER VON ERLACH (1656–1723) was the outstanding figure of the late Baroque in central Europe. He trained in sculpture and studied the works of Borromini and Bernini. His passion for the oval is evident in its use in his Castle Vranov (1690–94), with its oval windows and an oval vestibule, and also the Church of the Holy Trinity, in Salzburg (1694), which has a combination of transverse oval vestibule leading to a longitudinal oval interior. His best piece is the Karlskirche in Vienna (1716), where again, oval forms interlock with a Greek cross plan. The façade is extraordinary: much wider than

the building behind it and including two freestanding columns, copied from the Roman columns of Trajan and Marcus Aurelius, which rise above the façade to majestically frame the dome.

1755 Immanuel Kant (1724–1804) takes time off from philosophizing and points his great mind skyward. He posits the existence of conglomerates of stars called galaxies (galaxy is Greek for Milky Way).

1770 Captain Cook drops anchor at Botany Bay, as he names this bit of coastal Australia. Joseph Banks, one of his team of scientists, brings back plants for English greenhouses.

1783 The Mongolfier brothers take the first hot-air balloon for a flight.

Johann Lukas VON HILDEBRANDT (1688–1745) succeeded Fischer von Erlach as Court Architect in 1723. His Upper Belvedere in Vienna (1721–22) has a multitiered Oriental-fashion roof, common in central Europe. The Duan Kinksy Palace in Vienna (1713–16) is typical of his work, with delicate pilasters rising to great height on the façade, together with robust caryatids holding the open pediment over the entrance.

SOUTHERN GERMANY

Until the sixteenth century, staircases were usually utilitarian and generally hidden. However, later new types began to appear, with various landing configurations and open wells. The Baroque staircases of *Johann Balthasar NEUMANN* (1687–1753) exploited this new-found spatial possibility with fantastic paired sweeping curves, as at

the Episcopal Palace in Würzburg (1730). The plan for his hurch at Vierzenheiligen (1743) uses three intersecting ovals along the main axis of the nave, two circles at the transepts, and smaller ovals in the aisles. The effect of the undulating surfaces, decorated with white painted stucco lit by large windows, is dazzling.

Johann Michael FISCHER (1692–1766) was more prolific, completing as many as 32 churches and 22 abbeys. Still with the same rich stucco decorations, some of his buildings display a masterly spatial complexity. Two of the finest abbey churches are at Ottobeuren (1748–67) and

Architecture at the Crossroads...

...of Europe. Prague's Rococo legacy is a major one, and the Dientzenhoffer family had a controlling interest. You may need to know that Kilian Ignaz (1689–1751) was the most famous member of this tribe, a prolific church-builder who trained under Hildebrandt. His love of odd geometric shapes (octagons, ellipses) and domes permeated a huge output, but his older brother Johann (1663–1726) was more restrained (it comes with age). He's best known for Schloss Pommersfelden (1711–18), a richly stuccoed, exotically mirrored establishment (as only the Rococo knew how to create).

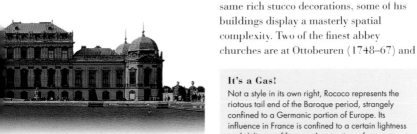

The Belvedere, Vienna (1693–1724), was built as a summer residence, with a lake and splendid gardens. This is the Upper Belvedere, separated from the lower buildings by magnificent gardens. The house is named after the belvedere—a look-out tower in the roof.

It's a Gas!

Not a style in its own right, Rococo represents the riotous tail end of the Baroque period, strangely confined to a Germanic portion of Europe. Its influence in France is confined to a certain lightness and delicacy of form on the exteriors of some buildings. A very few Rococo interiors are hidden away inside English houses, but beyond this, its impact is restricted to the garden, where determined investigators may spot garden furniture with Chinese, Indian, or Gothic overtones.

1653 Five-year-old Louis XIV comes to the throne in France.

1658 Faithorne publishes a fairly accurate map of London. Only eight years later the Great Fire of London renders it obsolete. Ogilvy, Morden, and Lea's new map will appear in 1682.

1665 Wren comes back from Paris full of ideas for city designs and plots a rash of rond-points and radiating avenues for London.

1600~1750

When Is an Architect not an Architect?

Sir Christopher Wren

Sir Christopher WREN (1632–1723) was a classicist, mathematician, and astronomer—and had no education as an architect. But he had studied the texts of Alberti, Serlio, and Palladio and met Mansart and a very old Bernini while in France. So the invitation to rebuild London after the Great Fire of 1666 was an inspired piece of visionary daring on the part of the City Fathers.

In Wren's church of St. Stephen Walbrook in London (1672–79), diagonal arches cut across the rectangular grid of columns to form an octagonal base for the hemispherical dome.

Wren produced a bold plan to replace the jumble of narrow streets and winding alleys with a new design of wide bulevards radiating from imposing squares. However, the reconstruction eventually followed the existing medieval street pattern. The rebuilding of London was rapid and included domestic and commercial buildings, 50 city churches, and Wren's universally known landmark, St. Paul's Cathedral.

The city churches were remarkable both in their form and their Classical appearance. Plans are simple; as Protestant churches, they had to have large spaces to accommodate congregational worship and the all-important pulpit. A whole variety of towers and tall spires allowed them to be easily identified in the dense urban area of the city of London.

St. Stephen, Walbrook (1672–87), has a rectangular plan, a regular grid of Corinthian columns, and an entablature in the form of a Greek cross supporting a dome. Wren thought his St. James, Piccadilly (1683), to be the ideal church—a simple rectangular plan with a timber barrel–vaulted ceiling. Galleries at each side are an integral part of the composition, forming a Doric base for the Corinthian order above.

ST. PAUL'S CATHEDRAL

St. Paul's Cathedral (1675–1710) marks a dramatic move away from the Catholic Gothic cathedrals and their intricate shadowy depths. The clear spaces and clean surfaces are starkly lit with clear glass in place of the colored glass of the Gothic. The original plan was to have been

1660 The restoration of the monarchy, and the founding of the Royal Society. Wren is a founding member.

1693 German philosopher and mathematician Wilhelm Leibnitz (1646–1716) toys with the binary system, based on two units and operating with the symbols 1 and 0. This is the basis of computer language.

1704–11 The early days of English journalism, with the publishing of the first editions of the *Review* (Daniel Defoe), the *Tattler* (Richard Steele) and the *Spectator* (Joseph Addison).

NAMES ON THE WALL

Roger North (1653–1734), *lawyer and sometime architect, wrote: "For a profest architect is proud, opiniative and troublesome, seldome at hand, and a head workman pretending to the designing part, is full of paultry vulgar contrivances; therefore be your owne architect, or sitt still." And* **Vanbrugh** *lists clients of* **William Talman** (1650–1719) *who sorely wished they had done the job themselves: the* **Dukes of Devonshire** *and* **Kingston; Lords Normanby, Coningsby,** *and* **Portmoor; Lady Falkland,** *and* **Sir John Germaine.** *All had met with nothing but "vexation and disappointment."*

'That Miracle of a Youth"

Thus said the English antiquarian John Evelyn of Sir Christopher Wren, then aged only 21, who ranks as the most remarkable architect of any generation. Wren was trained as a scientist, and his long life covered an epoch in which scientific discoveries paraleled appalling bloodletting in the English Civil War. As a demonstrator in anatomy at the College of Surgeons, or as a highly regarded geometrician, Wren led the field. The tremors of the Restoration and the Great Fire of London (1666) followed. St. Paul's Cathedral was his big chance to make his mark. He took it.

a Greek cross with a lengthened west arm, but the establishment preferred a Latin cross. The altar is no longer under the dome—the pulpit has taken its place at the crossing.

Externally, Wren's original idea was also abandoned: a proposed giant order was replaced by two levels of small columns, a motif that becomes a useful device as it continues all around the building. The upper level becomes a screen to hide the flying buttresses and pitched roofs. The dome is reminiscent of Bramante's Tempietto, Rome (1502), but at a vast scale. The most unusual, un-English aspects of the composition are the two flamboyant towers on the west façade, more characteristic of late Baroque in northern Europe.

Wren's masterpiece is St. Paul's Cathedral (1675–1710). Thirty-two radiating buttresses help to bear the weight of the central dome, which is crowned by a lantern, ball, and cross of enormous weight and is 366 feet/111.5 meters high.

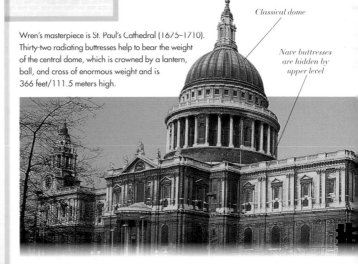

Classical dome

Nave buttresses are hidden by upper level

1669 Samuel Pepys writes the last page of his last diary and his coded record of London life since 1660, and all the dramas thereof await posterity. (Pepys dies in 1703.)

1679 Nicholas Hawksmoor is engaged by Wren as his personal clerk and is soon working for him in surveying and design.

1690 As an army captain, Vanbrugh is arrested in Calais and spends two years in prison (thought to be for spying).

1700~1750

English Baroque Revisited
Hawksmoor, Vanbrugh, and Gibbs

The great English building projects of the seventeenth century—St. Paul's Cathedral, Greenwich Hospital, and the City churches—were paid for by taxes levied by the Crown. The early eighteenth century brought new money and new patrons. Businessmen, with income from exploitation of the colonies, and wealthy landowners began to build.

Hawksmoor's Easton Neston (1697–1702) has unusual proportions—narrow, elongate windows and a one-bay portico

The dramatist *John VANBRUGH* (1664–1726), with no architectural training, became one of the leading country-house architects of the English Baroque style. His work uses massive forms, often grossly proportioned and heavy looking, unpopular with Classical purists but very powerful and distinctive. Castle Howard, in Yorkshire (1699–1712), bears a resemblance to French seventeenth-century planning as used at Versailles, with a *cour d'honneur* in front of the main house flanked by wings. Internal courtyards, *cours anglaises*, house the stables and kitchens. The grandiose scheme has a dome and a pedimented front.

Seaton Delaval (1720–28), in Northumberland, is unlike anything before it, resembling a massive medieval fortress.

Vanbrugh was commissioned by Queen Anne to build the magnificent Blenheim Palace (1705–24) for the Duke of Marlborough. It is seen as his finest achievement, with a combination of substantial-looking bold massing of the central block and wings, contrasting with a varied, picturesque skyline.

Castle Howard, in Yorkshire (1699–1712), was Sir John Vanbrugh's first architectural work. A whole village was demolished to provide the expansive site.

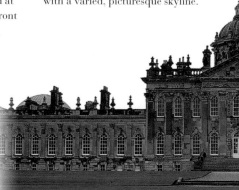

1698 Hawksmoor meets Vanbrugh, a successful and witty playwright, Whig, and rowdy member of the Kit-Cat Club, and converts the latter to architecture.

1704 John Churchill, Duke of Marlborough, trounces the French at the battle of Blenheim; the nation rewards him with Blenheim Palace, built at the taxpayer's expense.

The Ascot race meeting is established by Queen Anne, giving ladies their first opportunity to wear extravagant headgear.

NICHOLAS HAWKSMOOR

Nicholas HAWKSMOOR (1661–1736) started working in Wren's office at the age of 18. He assisted Vanbrugh at Castle Howard and Blenheim Palace. Unlike Wren and Vanbrugh, he didn't work at anything else, but devoted himself to architecture from the start, adopting a rigorous analytical approach, working with detailed drawings and abstract geometries. His best-known and most interesting works are his six City churches, built between 1711 and 1718 during his appointment as surveyor, under the

James Gibbs

Gibbs (1682–1754) was Hawksmoor's fellow surveyor at the Office of Works. His St. Mary le Strand (1714–17) is clearly in the Italian Mannerist style. St. Martin-in-the-Fields (1721–26) marks a dramatic change of style, with Palladian elements added to the Roman. The tower and steeple are now set back behind the pedimented portico, a relationship that, despite criticism, became standard. His name is now given to the distinctive, "rusticated" window surround previously used by Palladio at the Palazzo Thiene (1542).

Act for Building Fifty New Churches. Always based on skillfully designed axial plans and employing mass to create dramatic effect, all demonstrate an ingenious combination of Baroque, Classical, and Gothic elements.

At St. Mary, in Woolnoth (1716), a solid, rectilinear, rusticated tower stands apart from the main space with minimal surface articulation and tiny openings, supporting two square turrets. Christchurch, Spitalfields (1723–39) appears less solidly grounded with a precariously balanced spire above a thin tower. This is supported on a porch using the Palladian motif, on a large scale, and in three dimensions.

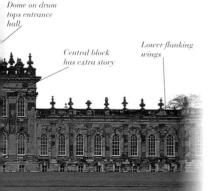

Dome on drum tops entrance hall

Central block has extra story

Lower flanking wings

1688 Polished glass manufactured on industrial scale in France. The new technology was already in place in Mansart's dazzling Galerie des Glaces (Hall of Mirrors,) built between 1678–84 at Versailles for Louis XIV.

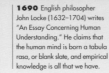

1690 English philosopher John Locke (1632–1704) writes "An Essay Concerning Human Understanding." He claims that the human mind is born a tabula rasa, or blank slate, and empirical knowledge is all that we have.

1706 Henry Mill invents carriage springs. Journeys around town become much more comfortable.

1715~50
Palladian Revival
Burlington, Campbell, and Kent

The Palladian revival was also a revival of the style of Inigo Jones. In England the style produced numerous domestic buildings inspired by and largely imitative

Chiswick House, in London, was designed by Lord Burlington with the assistance of William Kent in highly Italianate style.

Palladian house plans are typically geometric.

of the country houses of Palladio. Grand flights of steps sweep up to pedimented entrances on a raised main floor, above a rusticated semibasement. The planning is geometric, repetitive, and symmetrical, with different roof slopes and domes gently breaking up the solid mass of the building.

The name of *Richard BOYLE BURLINGTON* (1694–1753) is synonymous with the Palladian revival. An amateur architect himself, he was extremely influential as a patron. He also financed publications such as Palladio's drawings of Roman baths and Kent's *Designs of Inigo Jones*. His own villa at Chiswick (1725) was built in imitation of Palladio's Villa Rotonda to house his paintings and books. At the foot of the entrance stairs are statues of both Palladio and Inigo Jones. Burlington's rigid adherence to the rules of antiquity and his imitation of Palladio are evident in his other works, such as the ballroom at the Assembly Rooms, York (1731–32), copied from the Egyptian Halls of Palladio.

BURLINGTON'S BOYS

Colen CAMPBELL (1676–1729) started as a lawyer before publishing the first volume of *Vitruvius Britannicus* in 1715. Lord Burlington was so impressed with it that he fired Gibbs, who was working with him on Burlington House, and gave the job to Campbell instead. His Mereworth Castle, Kent (1723), is yet another version of the Villa Rotonda. Houghton Hall, built for the Prime Minister Robert Walpole (1723), has a central salon and cubic hall taken from Inigo Jones's Queen's House. The windows have rusticated "Gibbs surrounds," which were themselves already secondhand from Palladio's Palazzo Thiene, Vicenza (begun in 1542 but never actually completed).

1715 Lancelot "Capability" Brown, landscape gardener, born at Kirkharle, Northumberland. He will go on to develop the capabilities of Blenheim and Kew.

1742 Color printing developed in Japan. Kitagawa Utamaro (1753–1806) becomes the greatest exponent of the ukiyo-e (floating world) school of art, which focuses on the pleasures of life.

1749 Henry Fielding writes his masterpiece, *Tom Jones*, the picaresque adventures of a handsome young squire.

William KENT (1685–1748) was both a landscape gardener and architect, discovered by Burlington when he was studying painting in Rome (1719). His best work, Holkham Hall (1734), is an impressive catalog of elements of Palladianism, antiquity, and lavish Italian Baroque-inspired interiors. The plan has four identical wings arranged symmetrically around a central block. His last work is the Horse Guards in London (1750–58), which is very similar to Holkham

Campbell's Mereworth Castle, Kent, is another careful imitation of Palladio's Villa Rotonda.

Arcadia, Eh?

Art into Landscape or Landscape into Art? The eighteenth century saw The Grand Tour in full swing, and when the English milords weren't bringing back "cartloads of dead Christs and Madonnas" from Italia (thank you, William Hogarth), they took note of the painting of Nicolas Poussin (1594–1665) and the ex-pastry cook Claude Gellée, or Lorrain (1600–8?) Perfectly arranged landscapes. Palladian to a T. Someone has a bright idea. Why not make gardens like the pictures. Trees. Lakes. Templos. Many try, but the acknowledged garden king is Lancelot "Capability" Brown (1716–83), best known for horticultural wonders at Blenheim (1765) and elsewhere. Would-be initiates should see Stowe (Buckinghamshire) and Stourhead (Wiltshire).

Kent is more important as the originator of the English landscape garden and the beginnings of the idea of an architecture designed as part of a landscape rather than as a feature that dominates its environment.

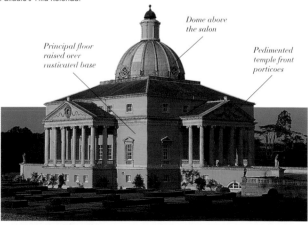

Dome above the salon

Principal floor raised over rusticated base

Pedimented temple front porticoes

1700s For English and European gentlemen, the Grand Tour of cities and archeological sites of Europe is de rigueur.

1717 Handel's *Water Music* is first performed on the Thames River. It was written for Handel's fellow German-turned-Englishman, George I.

1725 In cities, the sedan chair (introduced in the previous century) is now an established and popular means of transportation for the wealthy.

1720~1795

Adam Family Values
Georgian

The design ability and business acumen of the Adam family made them highly successful as property developers and interior designers. Between the rigors of the Palladian revival and the austerity of the Greek revival, the Adam style—much influenced by Italian and Roman buildings—is less ostentatious, calmer, finer, and more elegant. It is an altogether more delicate version of Neoclassicism.

Robert ADAM (1728–92) was convinced that the architect should take responsibility for the design of the interiors of buildings as well as the exterior. Consequently, he created interiors that have an unsurpassed level of complex and intricate decoration. Dry, white, chalky plaster moldings applied to surfaces painted in bold colors give otherwise flat surfaces a richness and depth. Often decorative patterns described in raised plaster moldings on the ceiling are repeated woven in carpets on the floor. Spaces are also richer—extended by niches, alcoves, or rows of freestanding columns with apses beyond.

Robert Adam had studied architecture along with his brothers James (1732–94) and John (1721–92) in his father's Edinburgh office. A tour of Europe (1754–58) gave him the opportunity to study the ancient Roman buildings, after which he settled in London, where he worked mostly on interiors of houses such as Kenwood (1767–69), Syon House, London (1760–69), and Osterly Park (1761–80). Kedleston Hall, in Derbyshire (1760–61), is a good example of his departure from the strictly Palladian. The plan, which was started

Stoned. Immaculate.
The Palladian and Neoclassical periods in Britain spawned new townscapes, notable for the use of stone in their building. New Georgian Bath and neighboring Clifton in Bristol are built with the lovely golden yellow local stuff; Edinburgh's New Town is elegantly gray granite, while Midlands chic is red sandstone. It's all kosher Neoclassical. Easy access to materials cut costs and provided the elegance desired by the architects, which marked the locations for life. Brick? You can't get much brickier than Georgian Bloomsbury. But it wasn't a universal trend, and stone was used wherever status takes a stand, such as Soane's Bank of England in the 1790s.

by *James PAINE* (1717–89)—not to mention previous architects whose plans had been rejected—is Palladian, very similar to Holkham Hall, in Norfolk (1734), and the main entrance façade uses the customary pedimented portico. Other elements are quite distinctly Roman: the south façade is modeled on the Arch of Constantine and fronts a salon with a Pantheonesque dome.

DOMESTIC PROJECTS

Adam designed several terraces of houses, including Charlotte Square in Edinburgh (1791–1807) and Fitzroy Square in London. Both have individual houses designed as part of a whole "palazzo" façade with a pedimented center. His earliest terrace was the Adelphi (1768–72, demolished 1937), a speculative development that included stables, offices, and warehouses as well as residences. Built on the banks of the Thames, it used the sloped ground to advantage for access

The library at Kenwood House, London (1767–69), is characteristic of Robert Adam's interiors.

roads from the Strand at first-floor level, above the "rustic" arched colonnaded wharf area at river level. The façade was of painted stucco with the usual applied decorative motifs and a giant order of pilasters. The project was a financial disaster, leaving Adam without work for several years.

The north façade of Kedleston Hall in Derbyshire, England (1757–70), designed in a Palladian manner.

Putting on the Style

Want a British architect you can call a truly European figure? Try Robert Adam. His many achievements included decor developed with what nowadays would be called "a market" in mind: those who were actively seeking new forms of Classicism. Adam's furnishings were enormously detailed. On the walls of his rooms, comfortable pastel colors; Etruscan motifs; on the floors, marble; and the fireplaces, which bear his name, have mantelpieces supported on miniature columns. Outside, the lovely landscape gardens of the picturesque. Nothing could be more pleasing to the eye.

1811 John Nash, recently married to a lady said to be the mistress of the Prince Regent, is commissioned to design Regent's Park, with its terraces, villas, and picturesque lakes.

1812 The Elgin marbles are taken to England by Thomas Bruce, the seventh earl of Elgin.

1813 In the ballrooms of Europe the waltz is being danced by dashing army captains and blushing ladies.

1790~1840

Manly Virtues
Greek Revival

Substantial columns, Doric capitals, and flat stucco work

Neoclassicism was a definite reaction to the earlier excesses of Baroque and also to the increasingly fashionable, picturesque Neo-Gothic. Both of these styles looked back to the past "when life was simpler," Gothic to the medieval past and Neoclassical right back to ancient Rome and Greece. The earliest, the Greek Doric order, answered the search for purity; it was the simplest and the most "masculine." Two chaps in particular were in the vanguard: Sir John Soane and John Nash.

Park Crescent, Regents Park, in Lon[don] (1812–22), is a simple semicircul[ar] façade framing Portland Place, leading to Regent Street.

Soane's churches

Two London churches in particular show Soane's rigorous pursuit of purity of form. The west façade of St. John's has a pediment and no portico; the piers flanking the entrance simply rise up past the cornice line to form the base of the square tower. At St. Peter's, Walworth, the façade is uninterrupted, with the Ionic columns of the porch recessed. The frieze, with a relief Greek key pattern, continues across, emphasizing the horizontality of the main space in contrast to the very tall steeple.

Sir John SOANE'S (1753–1837) architecture has a distinct originality. Unlike earlier copied "styles" it is best described as an abstraction of Classicism. Particular elements are continually developed in his work: the spatial potential of walls is explored through multiple layers and recesses; surfaces are free from fussy decorations; and any applied

NAMES ON THE WALL

Humphrey Repton *(1752–1818) followed in the wake of* **Lancelot "Capability" Brown**, *but it was he who invented the term landscape gardening. He was a country gentleman obliged to earn a living from his passion for horticulture. Although not averse to architectural endeavor, he had an arrangement with* **Nash** *whereby work of this kind was turned over to him for a small percentage commission. About two hundred gardens and parks received Repton's attention, and he was mentioned by name in* **Jane Austen's** *Mansfield Park.*

1814 Gas is used for public streetlighting for the first time. Westminster in London is now lit up at night.

1815 At the Battle of Waterloo the Duke of Wellington's troops rout Napoleon's army.

1820 The Danish physicist Hans Oersted notices that an electric current deflects a compass needle, and electromagnetism is discovered.

moldings are of minimal depth or contained within the surface. Daylight is manipulated to create dramatic effect and illusion. In common with architects of the Baroque, the sensual spatial experience is as important as visual harmony and geometric logic. The dramatic effects are the result of manipulation of volume and light rather than form and decoration.

Soane's own house in Lincoln's Inn, in London (1812), is a wonderful example of his work. On an ordinary-sized terraced house plot, magical spaces unfold, every wall is several layers deep, and a whole forest of lanterns, hidden above roof level, allow the daylight to penetrate deep into the plan.

Follies

Mock ruins in a country park, intended to delight, are the most straightforward follies. Expensive but fun, and if you were clever you might make use of them. Grottoes, like the one at Stourhead. A tower, like that at Cothele, Devon. But if you were an eccentric millionaire with an interest in architecture like William Beckford (1760–1844,) you might build a Gothic abbey (1796–1807) based on Salisbury Cathedral with a horrendously high tower. It falls (to no one's surprise) in 1825.

Shropshire (1806), in an equally picturesque Italian vernacular style. His Brighton Pavilion (1802–21) is in an oriental style replete with onion domes and minarets. His most interesting work, for its size and ingenuity, is the planning of an area of London (1811 onward), including Regents Park and Portland Place, Regent Street, and down to Carlton House Terrace, taking in All Souls Church at Langham Place (1822–25). The design of the terraces that line the park is unadventurous, using a mixture of all the Neoclassical elements available. The most interesting is Park Crescent at the top of Portland Place, which has the simplest of façades, with flat stucco work and paired Ionic columns, and the boldest form

DEDICATED FOLLOWER OF FASHION

In contrast to Soane's pursuit of individuality, *John Nash* (1752–1835) was a follower of fashion who would do anything in any style. As a country house architect he designed Luscombe Castle, in Devon (1800–04), an asymmetrically planned Gothic castle, and Cronkhill, in

Soane's house at Lincoln's Inn Fields, in London (1812). The bay window at first floor level was originally an open loggia

1751 Denis Diderot (1713–84) publishes the first chunk of his encyclopedia (from the Greek words meaning general education), an attempt to summarize human knowledge.

1773 American colonists dump cargoes of East India tea into the sea at Boston harbor (the Boston Tea Party) in protest against British monopolies and taxes.

1781 In Yorktown, Virginia, General Cornwallis surrenders to George Washington. The redcoats are marched away as the military band plays on.

1790~1840

Oh Those Greeks
Greek Revival 2

The fashion for reviving primitive Greek architecture became firmly established in the late eighteenth century, and stepped out boldly from its British stronghold. "Plain, sturdy and masculine," with its geometric forms and absence of decoration, it provided an alternative to the picturesque Gothic revival, as well as tying in with contemporary Neoclassicists.

Thomas JEFFERSON (1743–1826), the third president of the United States, as well as being an economist and educationalist, was a successful and influential architect. He had visited Europe and based his work on drawings in Palladio's *Quattro Libri* and in Robert Morris's book *Select Architecture*.

His design for the Virginia State Capitol, his first Neoclassical building in the U.S., became the model for state architecture to follow. He was involved in the planning of Washington, D.C., and the new University of Virginia (1817). The axial rectilinear lawn, with porticoed villas on the long sides, and the principal building at one end, became the model for university campuses.

Benjamin Henry LATROBE (1764–1820) had worked in England for Cockerell as an architect and for Smeaton as an engineer before emigrating to the U.S. and working for Jefferson. His Bank of Pennsylvania

> ### NAMES ON THE WALL
>
> **James "Athenian" Stuart** *(1713–88) and* **Nicholas Revett** *(1720–1804) are considered to be the instigators of Greek revivalism in England, following their four-year sojourn in Greece and the publication of* Antiquities of Athens *in 1762.* **Sir Robert Smirke** *(1780–1876) introduced the style with his Covent Garden Theatre (1808, demolished), the first Greek Doric building in London. This successful architect's best-known building is the British Museum, London (1823–47), with its huge scale and imposing Greek manner.*

The Top German
Karl Friedrich Schinkel (1781–1841) was the greatest architect in Germany in the Neoclassical period. He studied under Gilly (1772–1800) and became head of the Public Works Department in Prussia in 1830. He completed many prestigious public buildings, especially in Berlin, in the Greek revival style, such as the New Guard House (1816–18) and the Schauspielhaus (1819–21). The Altes Museum has a mural in the Doric portico and an unusual interior that includes a central dome. Schinkel's most exquisite buildings are the Charlottenburg, in Berlin (1824–25), with perfect geometry of smooth walls and deeply recessed loggias, and in contrast the asymmetrical arrangements of two simple, almost bucolic, buildings, the Charlottenhof (1826) and the Roman Bathhouse (1833) in the park at Potsdam.

1783 The British recognize American independence in the Treaty of Paris, and the Revolutionary War ends.

1787 The United States introduces the currency of the dollar. Coinage is minted in 1792.

1789 An overtaxed bourgeoisie and disgruntled peasantry form an unlikely alliance and instigate the French Revolution. Three years later France is declared a republic.

(1799–1801) and the Water Works (1800) in Philadelphia established the Greek revival in the U.S. Baltimore Cathedral (1804–18), probably influenced by Soane's work, is his best. It has a shallow dome, an elongated nave, and fine vaulting.

FRANCE

The work of *Etienne-Louis BOULLÉE* (1728 –99) and *Claude-Nicolas LEDOUX* (1736–1806) takes Neoclassicism to its extreme. Fascinating in its combination of logic, it couples the simple forms of pure geometries with an emotive expressionism. Boullée's proposed monument for Isaac Newton (1784), a vast, 492 feet/150 meter-high sphere rising from a drum that symbolizes the heavens, demonstrates his belief that architecture should express character and magic as well as reason.

While most of Boullée's work remained on paper, Ledoux's was built. The Barrière de la Villette (1785–89), one of the remaining toll gates to Paris, is in the pure form of a Greek cross and cylinder, intended to communicate the dominance and affluence of the city. The saltworks at Arc-et-Senans (1775–79) is the only built part of his visionary city of Chaux, and has some unusual combinations of classical motifs. Unfluted Greek Doric columns of chunky proportions stand at the entrance— a massive arch leading to a grottolike tunnel.

The University of Virginia (1017), Thomas Jefferson. Each building was a Classical copy as an example to the students.

Steps emphasize focal point

The rotunda is copied from the Pantheon in Rome

The Greeks in Scotland

William Henry Playfair (1790–1857), with Thomas Hamilton (1784–1858), led the Greek revival in Edinburgh, The Ionic National Gallery of Scotland (1850) and the Doric Royal Scottish Academy (1822) are Playfair's best-known works. Alexander "Greek" Thomson (1817–75), working 30 years later, built several enchanting churches in Glasgow, combining the purity of form and absence of decoration with an intriguing originality of composition. The Caledonia Road Church (1856) has an immaculate Ionic portico on top of a solid base.

1829 An instrument from China known as the sheng is introduced to Vienna. In English-speaking countries it will soon be known as the mouth organ.

1837 In France the Commission for Historic Monuments is created, with a mission to restore medieval buildings, despite opposition from the Neoclassicists.

1840s Gaslight is now found in all the better city houses.

1800~1900

Aspirations
Gothic Revival

The picturesque skyline and the pointed arches, steeples, and pinnacles of the Palace of Westminster represented a triumph for the Neo-Gothic over the Neoclassical when it was built in the middle of the nineteenth century. Architects and patrons until then had been preoccupied with the Neoclassical style, which was firmly established as appropriate for important institutions. Gothic was acceptable for religious buildings.

Barry's Westminster New Palace, London (1836–68) —the Houses of Parliament to you and me—is the first significant Gothic Revival building. The authentic Gothic detail was provided by A.W.N. Pugin.

The Rijksmuseum, Amsterdam (1877–85), by Petrus Cuijpers, is a Dutch version of secular Gothic with steeply pitched roofs and rib vaulting.

A fire in 1834 destroyed the medieval Palace of Westminster, except for the Great Hall. For the replacement palace buildings, it was decided to choose Gothic rather than the prevailing fashionable Neoclassical, to be more in keeping with the remaining medieval buildings. The plans of *Charles Barry* (1785–1860), a confirmed Neoclassicist, were accepted and *Augustus Welby Pugin* (1812–52) provided the Gothic influence. Barry's plan was along Classical lines with symmetrical façades; the Gothic embellishments—the pointed arches and *flêches* (spires)—were added by Pugin, a devout Catholic who saw a direct connection between religious faith and the Gothic cathedrals, more particularly the most elaborate "second pointed" style of the thirteenth and fourteenth centuries.

1843 Pugin takes to striding around the coastal town of Ramsgate in eccentric sailor's costume and long boots, looking out to sea.

1848 The Pre-Raphaelite Brotherhood is founded in England, with a mission to restore the purity of fifteenth-century Italian work to contemporary painting.

1881 The world has its first electric tram, which operates in Berlin.

NAMES ON THE WALL

Structural analysis by the French theorist **Eugène-Emmanuel Viollet-le-Duc** *(1814–79), in* Dictionnaire Raisonné de l'Architecture Française *(1854–68), demonstrated that Gothic architecture was rational, constructed in a logical way, in accordance with the natural laws of structures and gravity. In a later work,* Entretiens, *he made comparisons with the contemporary skeleton structures developed along rational lines by engineers. Viollet-le-Duc was responsible for reinstating the statues of the "Kings of Judah and Israel" on the façade of Notre Dame in Paris; they were destroyed in 1793 in the belief that they represented the French monarchy.*

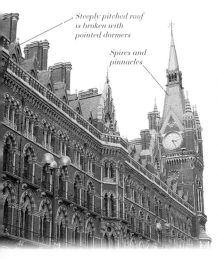

Sir George Gilbert Scott's St. Pancras Station building, with its hotel (1865–71), is one of London's High Victorian Gothic glories.

Steeply pitched roof is broken with pointed dormers

Spires and pinnacles

PREACHING TO THE CONVERTED

The Gothic revival had already begun to be fashionable at the end of the eighteenth century. Horace Walpole had his house Strawberry Hill rebuilt in eclectic Gothic style (1749–76). But it was the Palace of Westminster that confirmed that the new Gothic—the Gothic revival—had at last been accepted for secular buildings. Other notable Gothic revival buildings in Britain include the Midland Hotel (1865), shielding St. Pancras from view, and Glasgow University (1866–71), both by *Sir George* GILBERT SCOTT (1811–78), and the Law Courts, London (1866–85), by *G. E.* STREET (1824–81). In Europe, the Houses of Parliament in Budapest (1883–1901) by *Imre* STEINDL (1839–1902) was built in imitation of the Palace of Westminster, and the Rijksmuseum in Amsterdam (1877) by *Petrus* CUIJPERS (1827–1921) is another example of the style.

True Principals

Augustus Pugin and John Ruskin (1819–1900) were the leading lights in art and architecture in Victorian England. Pugin's Catholic passion for the Gothic has already been mentioned. He is widely credited with having been the linchpin of the Gothic revival. As for Ruskin, this weirdo had a claw-like grip on the art of his day. In *The Seven Lamps of Architecture* (1849), he declared for Sacrifice, Truth, Power, Beauty, Life, Memory, and Obedience ("we want no new style … the forms of architecture already known are good enough for us"). But in his later book, *The Stones of Venice* (1851–53), this manic-depressive talked up the Venetian Gothic style and the earliest English decorated style. Small wonder that British building was such a mess.

1777–79 The first iron bridge is built at Coalbrookdale. It was designed by Abraham Darby, the first person to use coke instead of charcoal for producing cast iron.

1782 The improved steam engine is patented by James Watt. The water wheel of human history is at last effectively replaced and the Industrial Revolution is poised to begin.

1818 John Nash uses cast iron in the construction of the Royal Pavilion at Brighton.

1830~1900

The Iron Age
Iron and Steel

Architects, being as they were preoccupied with style, were slow to grasp the possibilities offered by new building techniques. It was engineers, excited by the potential of iron and steel, who first developed structural uses for the new materials. Joseph Paxton's Crystal Palace was the turning point that aroused architectural interest in these materials.

Built to house the Great Exhibition of 1851 in Hyde Park, London, the Crystal Palace took just nine months to erect. It was pioneering in its use of iron and was assembled on the site from a series of prefabricated panels. Built around existing trees, it was enormous, measuring 410 x 197 feet/125 x 60 meters in plan and 72 feet/22 meters in height. The structure's novel spatial effect was heightened by its almost complete transparency.

BUILDING BRIDGES

Cast iron had first been used structurally in England in 1779 for a bridge at Coalbrookdale, as well as for bridges in the U.S. and in France. The intense competition between the new railroad companies spurred bridge building as well as production of rails, which were also the first source of I-beams used in buildings. *Thomas Telford* (1757–1834) was the first to build arched bridges in cast iron, a material that works well in compression. Wrought iron, which works better in tension, he used for the chains on the suspension bridge over the Menai Straits (1819). Robert Stephenson's Britannia railroad bridge, also across the Menai (1850), used an innovative system of box girders made of wrought iron.

London's Crystal Palace was built for the Great Exhibition of 1851 and destroyed by fire in 1936.

1819–25 The building of the Menai Straits suspension bridge, by Telford, which has a span of 530 feet.

1825 England becomes the first country to have a railroad, with the opening of the Stockton-to-Darlington line.

1842 The first modern anesthetic (ether) is used by Crawford Long for the removal of a tumor in the neck of a patient (in the United States of America).

NAMES ON THE WALL

*The youngest, laziest, but also best trained of three **Cubitt** brothers, **Lewis** was assisted in his Kings Cross designs by middle brother **Joseph**. The eldest, **Thomas**, was the first of a new breed of building contractor. Employing craftsmen of all kinds on a permanent basis, he undertook building work on a scale previously unknown and developed land on his own account. Interested in smoke, sewage, parks, and public amenities, he also served as guarantor for that other constructional tour de force, the Great Exhibition of 1851, when support for it began to wobble.*

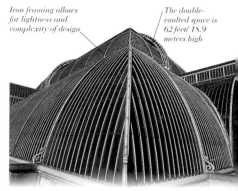

Iron framing allows for lightness and complexity of design

The double-vaulted space is 62 feet/ 18.9 meters high

The lofty transparent enclosure of the Palm House at the Royal Botanic Gardens, Kew, in London (1845–47), designed by Decimus Burton and Richard Taylor, can only hint at the interior of the Crystal Palace.

BUT IS IT ARCHITECTURE?

Iron was first used for warehouses, factories, and market halls, new building types in the nineteenth century, and it was some time before it was used for conventional buildings. Train sheds at railroad termini produced some of the most daring structures—dramatic spaces with huge spans, tall slender columns, and elaborate ironwork. The railroad companies' lack of confidence in the esthetic quality of such adventurous structures meant that many of these "utilitarian" spaces were concealed. Gothic, Tudor, and Greek revival ticket halls, hotels, and façades shielded the iron structures from public view as at Paddington (1852), St. Pancras (1865),

and Euston (1840). Kings Cross, London (1850), is an exception. Designed by Lewis Cubitt, it has a simple brick structure with two semicircular arches following the line of the train sheds behind. The only revivalist concession is the Italianate tower.

Glass houses, etc....

Continuing in the ground-breaking mold of the Crystal Palace, to demonstrate a nation's pride and identity and to demonstrate skill and prowess in construction and engineering, exhibition pavilions have continued to produce some great architectural and technological achievements. The Paris Exhibition of 1889 saw both the widest span and the tallest structure of the time. The Galerie des Machines, with huge portal frames hinged at the base and the apex, had the widest span at 394 feet/120 meters. The tallest was the Eiffel Tower, still standing on axis with the buildings at the Trocadéro, left from the Exhibition of 1878. Both Victor Contamin and Gustave Eiffel were heavily criticized by others who thought their daring steel constructions foolhardy.

1850~1950
The Hard Men
Concrete Structures

Reinforced concrete, which has had such dramatic effect on structure, form, and esthetics in the twentieth century, has its roots in the nineteenth century, and its development was closely linked with developments in steel technology.

The flats at 25b rue Franklin, Paris (1903), one of Auguste Perret's first works.

Concrete started to be used again in the late eighteenth century in France, and by the mid-nineteenth century it was routinely used in foundations and floors. Concrete—a mixture of sand, stones, and water—works well in compression (it can support heavy vertical loads). Experimentation with cast iron and then later steel bars resulted in a material that works well in compression and in tension, with the added advantage of being fire resistant. The sewers designed by *François Coignet* (1814–88) for Haussmann's Paris were among the first experiments to try out the potential of the new technology.

MAKING THE CONNECTION
The real breakthrough came when *François Hennebique* (1842–1921), another Frenchman, solved the problem of joints between columns and beams by using round reinforcing bars that could be bent and hooked together to form monolithic joints, enabling large-scale framed structures to be built. The name of François Hennebique rapidly became synonymous with reinforced concrete building work all over Europe.

NAMES ON THE WALL

Tony Garnier *graduated from the École des Beaux-Arts, winning the Prix de Rome in 1899. Instead of sketching antiquities,* **Garnier** *spent his time there working on his* Cité Industrielle. *Published in 1917, it was one of the earliest examples of city planning with fully thought-out zoning, but was also intended to be constructed primarily in concrete. The absolute geometric simplicity of many of his proposed buildings prefigures the little white boxes so beloved of Modern movement architects.*

1925 At the trend-setting Paris Exhibition of Decorative Arts the flavor of the day is things simple and plain. Designs are geometrical, cubist, or abstract, stylized developments of floral art nouveau.

1936 The Spanish Civil War breaks out.

1947 Television sets appear in more affluent homes.

Slim and Elegant

Felix Candela (1910–), a concrete engineer working in Mexico, is a key figure in the development of graceful, thin-skinned concrete shell structures using hyberbolic paraboloids; the first was the Cosmic Ray Building (1951), with roof as thin as ⅜ of an inch. Constructed using straight shutter boards, it has delicate curving shapes that are relatively simple and economical to produce. Working with different architects, Candela is known best for the Olympic Stadium in Mexico City (1968) and the church of Santa Maria Miraculosa, Mexico City (1954).

Perret's Church of Notre Dame, Le Raincy (1922–23) was instrumental in persuading France that concrete was an acceptable building material.

August PERRET (1874-1954) was one of the first architects to employ an all-concrete structure. In his apartment block on the rue Franklin in Paris (1903), the framed construction is made visible on the façade with infill of either windows or panels of ceramic tiling. The unusual concave form of the façade, a pragmatic response to gain more floor space by putting the obligatory "rear courtyard" at the front, adds to the "Gothic" impression created by the tall articulated form.

By the first decades of the twentieth century, frame structures of reinforced concrete had become standard. Future developments were in refinements of shape and surface texture and in other structural forms like the hyperbolic paraboloids of Freysinet's (1879–1962) airship hangars or the thin-skin shell structures of Perluigi Nervi (1891–1971). The most important aspect of monolithic framed construction to the early modern architects was the possibility of cantilevering the edge of floor slabs away from the columns to allow fully glazed façades.

All Modern Conveniences

From 1860 to 1890 Britain went through huge technological and social changes. Acts of parliament heralded slum destruction and a greater emphasis on public health, but buildings themselves reflected all sorts of new ideas... A contemporary Londoner might reflect "We've had Sir Joseph Bazalgette's (1819–91) sewerage system for the whole of London since the mid-1860s. That lavatory was fitted as standard some time after 1880. Lighting? We used gas for years (our stupid neighbors used it for ages), but when we saw electric light at the Savoy in 1881 I told the memsahib we had to have it whatever the cost. I know that the Sassoon and Rothschild houses in Brighton installed their own generators. And when we're at the club and a little the worse for wear, how do you think we climb all those stairs? We don't. We use those nice American lifts, or elevators, which have been just the thing since the 1860s. Pretty soon we'll buy one for the house as well...."

1865 The world's first political socialist party is officially born in Germany—the Social Democratic Labor Party.

1876 At the Centennial Show at Philadelphia is a display of Shaker furniture, and the fashion has been growing ever since.

1881 William Morris establishes his wallpaper and carpet factory in Merton. The wool is washed in the Wandle River before being dyed with Morris's own dyes and by his own hand.

1860~1900

Useful and Beautiful
Arts and Crafts

The Red House in Bexleyheath, Kent, was built by Philip Webb for William Morris in 1859–60 in an eclectic and informal Gothic design.

The Arts and Crafts movement developed in England in the late nineteenth century as a reaction against the arrival of machine-made mass production techniques, the results of which were shoddy and ugly. Its intention was to revive craftsmanship generally and in architecture to promote traditional building techniques using local materials.

William MORRIS (1834–96), the most influential figure in the movement, was a designer, a lecturer, a socialist, and a promoter of vernacular architecture. Art, for Morris, was part of life—not the domain of the rich elite: "I do not want art for a few any more than education for a few or freedom for a few." Frustrated by the difficulty in obtaining good-quality, well-designed products, in 1861 Morris set up his own company, Morris, Marshall and Faulkner (later Morris and Co.). His designs for wallpapers and fabric are often highly colored and intricately decorated, featuring birds and flowers. His call for better design and handicraft was influenced by the writings of Ruskin and his belief that quality came from the relationship between a craftsman and his

work, that labor should be a pleasurable activity. He thought that mass production produced ugly goods, and in separating the maker from the product of his labor, created a wage-dependent working class. By the 1890s, the movement had spread to Europe and North America.

One of the most influential buildings was Red House at Bexleyheath (1859), designed for Morris by his architect and friend *Philip WEBB* (1831–1915). Red House is an asymmetrical, free-plan composition, built in red brick (hence its name), with half-hipped roofs and rustic tiles—very different from the fashionable white-stuccoed "Italianate" villas. Morris went to town on the interior, reworking everything thoroughly—the wall hangings, furniture, and stained-glass windows.

1884 In Chicago, the first skyscraper is built: the Home Assurance Building by Jenney and Mundie.

1871–96 A string of comic operettas by Gilbert the librettist and the composer Sullivan is performed to enthusiastic audiences at the D'Oyly Carte Theatre, Sadlers Wells, London.

1897 Marconi uses kites and balloons to keep his receiver aerials aloft, and wireless communication is demonstrated on Salisbury Plain.

NAMES ON THE WALL

Sir Edward Burne-Jones *(1833–98) is probably best known because of his associations with the Pre-Raphaelite Brethren. His rise from freelance illustrator to a Baronetcy was not uncommon among his later circle, but in this context we have to see him as a major tapestry artist for Morris & Co. Not what you'd call the best draftsman of his era, Burne-Jones remains famous for his dull, "greenery-yallery" imitations of Botticelli. Like him or loathe him, he's still around.*

DUTCH DOMESTICITY

Richard Norman SHAW (1831–1912) represents the other strand of English country house architecture of the period. His early work is in the picturesque Gothic revival style. Leyswood, in Sussex (1868), and Cragside, in Northumberland (1870), are in a romantic, "old English" style. He later adopted the "Queen Anne" style, the quintessential English style, in a series of London town houses: flat red brick, staggered stone quoins, and hipped roofs— a revival of mid-seventeenth century brick buildings, reminiscent of Dutch architecture. This work previewed the Arts and Crafts he later adopted.

New Scotland Yard (1887–90), built of red brick with stone dressings, and elaborated with distinctive circular turrets, corbelled out at the corners, was his first public building.

Hey! What D'You Think You're Doing?

The Victorians also faced problems of conservation. After all, acid rain was there even if they didn't know what it was called, and most of the medieval buildings they knew were in states of considerable disrepair. So disrepaired, in fact, that contemporaries were conserving on a wing and a prayer. Sir George Gilbert Scott (1811–78), architect of churches, railroad stations, and civic and government buildings, was one of the worst of these well-meaning offenders: in his hands old buildings just lost all their *je ne sais quoi* beneath a veil of Victorian bilge. So, the Society for the Preservation of Ancient Buildings was formed in 1877, under the influence of (you guessed) Morris, to try and stop the rot. Definitely a good move, and inextricably associated with the Arts and Crafts Movement.

Bedford Park, in Chiswick, London, was a pioneering and influential "Queen Anne"-style suburb of the 1870s and 1880s, with houses, an inn, clubhouse, church, and studios designed by a number of major architects as an "esthetic Elysium."

1886 American Charles Hall (1863–1914) and French metallurgist Paul Heroult (1863–1914) perfect the way of making aluminum using an electric current passed through a solution of aluminum oxide. Aluminum becomes a cheap structural material.

1888 George Eastman (1854–1932) invents the Kodak camera. Home movies are born.

1889 In Paris, the Eiffel Tower is erected as a temporary structure (amid great protest) to demonstrate the latest building technology.

Late 19th Century

Home Sweet Home
Domestic Revival

The German architectural theorist Hermann Muthesius, in his book The English House *(1904), remarked that there was "nothing as unique and outstanding in English architecture as the development of the house." Architects in England as in Europe saw the necessity for a unique, regional, or national style as an alternative to the tide of revivalism and historicism. The vernacular traditions of the country house, together with the Arts and Crafts principles, was a way to achieve this.*

NAMES ON THE WALL

George Edmund Street *(1824–81). It's all his fault. If he hadn't been so successful and opened an architectural practice in Oxford in 1852, he probably wouldn't have trained Morris and Webb. But he did both, and as far as those two are concerned the rest is history. Street studied under Sir George Gilbert Scott , and traveled widely (Spain, Germany, and Italy), so it's not especially surprising that his use of the Gothic—the style of the day—has European leanings. Following many important church commissions, his important competition design for the Royal Courts of Justice of 1874–82 was completed by his son. Street was a great borrower of styles (even though they were all medieval), and happily talked up the idea of moving freely within them.*

Annesley Lodge, in London (1896), with its buttresses, white pebble-dashed walls, and long, red tiled roof, has all the elements that typify Voysey's domestic style.

The vernacular tradition of building is related to physical conditions (climate, landscape, and local materials) and the complex social structures of late Victorian England. This is exemplified in the work of C. F. A. VOYSEY (1857–1941), a leading proponent of the Arts and Crafts domestic revival in England and a prolific builder of houses. His country houses are distinctive: long and low with horizontal windows, steeply pitched roofs, and white-painted, rough-finished plaster walls. The Orchard, in Chorley Wood (1899), is a typical example. His interiors, with white paneling and delicate colors, have come to represent a "feminine," cozy image.

1900 Pierre Bonnard (1867–1947) and Édouard Vuillard (1868–1940) begin to record the beauties of domestic life; they form what is known as the Intimiste school.

1900 Sigmund Freud brings out *The Interpretation of Dreams,* based on his clinical experience in Vienna.

1920 Radio broadcasting begins on a regular basis in the U.S.

PASSING ON THE MESSAGE

William Richard LETHABY (1857–1931) completed very few buildings, but they are immensely important. The church of All Saints in Brockhampton (1900–02) is one of the most original buildings of its time, and other buildings include Avon Tyrrell, in Hampshire (1891), and Melsetter House, in Orkney (1898). Lethaby was the first director of the Central School of Arts and Crafts—the first school to include workshops for teaching crafts. Lethaby's influence as a scholar and a teacher has been wide-reaching. His *History of Architecture* (1898) is confirmation of the Arts and Crafts principles that "design… is as nothing compared to workmanship" and "design should not be a matter of scholarship, knowledge of historical styles, but a response to immediate needs."

Sir Edward Lutyens

Influenced by Shaw and Webb, Sir Edward Lutyens (1869–1944) designed some of the best-known English country houses in a style linked to the Arts and Crafts movement. For example, he created Deanery Garde at Sonning, in Berkshire (1899–1902), and Munstead Wood at Godalming, in Surrey, for Gertrude Jekyll. He went on to design commercial buildings in London, such as the Midland Bank headquarters (1924–39) and Britannic House (1920–24), as well as the plan for New Delhi. Another Arts and Crafts exponent was Hugh Mackay Baillie Scott (1865–1945), who was interested in socialist ideas for alternative forms of dwelling, collective living arrangements, and alternatives to the family house, especially as women became more independent. At Hampstead Garden Suburb in London, he designed Waterlow Court, an apartment building for single women that operated on a collective basis, with a shared kitchen and laundry and rooms arranged around a closed quadrangle for exercising.

No Pictures Please!

W. R. Lethaby (1857–1931) formed the Art Workers' Guild in 1884. He wanted to bring all kinds of craftsmen together who did not call themselves institutionalized, and their initial membership included a mixed group of imaginative bodies called The Fifteen. The AWG saw themselves as the custodians of taste …but they didn't want to talk about their "Great and Improving Efforts on Behalf of Society." Strange! Because of this the Arts and Crafts Exhibition Society was formed to hold the exhibitions the AWG didn't want! Both organizations would clash with a new tendency in design, Art Nouveau, a story that unfolds biomorphically elsewhere.

Traditional thatch

Local stone

All Saints, Lethaby's church at Brockhampton, was built in true Arts and Crafts manner.

1895 *The Studio* magazine holds a competition for the design of the "Ideal Coal Scuttle." One of the entrants is M. H. Baillie Scott.

1895 A shop named "Art Nouveau" opens in Paris, aiming to sell objects of completely modern, nonimitative design.

1890s Ragtime is all the rage in New York. Scott Joplin's syncopated rhythms are heard all over town.

1890~1905
Follow the Curve
Art Nouveau

Art Nouveau originated in two-dimensional graphic and textile design in the 1880s and spread to furniture and architecture in the 1890s. In common with the Arts and Crafts movement, Art Nouveau rejected historicism and adopted ideas of truth to materials and the value of craftsmanship. However, while Arts and Crafts tended to look back to a medieval past as its model, Art Nouveau looked forward to the potential of new building technologies and wealth made possible through the use of new production techniques.

The entrance to the Porte Dauphine métro station in Paris (c.1900) is typical of the arresting Art Nouveau designs of Hector Guimard.

The "New Free Style" based on organic forms and inspired by nature was associated with youth, freedom, and purity. It spread across most of Europe, known by different names—*Jugendstil* in German and *Stile Liberte* in Italian—but it remains most closely associated with Belgium and France, as Art Nouveau.

Art Nouveau's association with the applied arts and fin de siècle decadence, together with its obvious glamorizing intent, has led to its often being dismissed by theorists and historians as merely decoration. In fact, the long, languorous curves and slender stalks of Art Nouveau were ideally suited to the new metal-working technologies and were able to exploit the potential of materials such as wrought iron in a simultaneous expression of structure and decoration.

1895–1900 Victor Horta, a Belgian baron, is building the Hotel Solvay and Van Eetvelde house in Brussels, replete with sinuous, flowing linear decoration using stylized plant forms.

1900 German physicist Max Planck proposes the theory that energy is "composed" of indivisible units, and the Quantum Theory—and modern physics—is born.

1903 Founded: the Wiener Werkstätte, for architects and artists following the principles of William Morris.

NAMES ON THE WALL

Arthur Heygale Mackmurdo *(1851–1942) is credited with the first Art Nouveau curves on book covers for his Wren's City churches (1884) and Century Guild (1882).* **Odon Lechner** *(1845–1914) built the Postal Savings Bank, Budapest (1899–1902), with decorative Dutch gables and vernacular motifs.* **Henri van de Velde** *(1863–1957) became a successful designer under the influence of Ruskin and Morris, designing his first house in 1892. He became director of the School of Arts and Crafts in Berlin.*

VIVE LA FRANCE

Hector GUIMARD (1867–1942) based his work on three principles drawn from the "big book" of nature—logic, harmony, and sentiment—and was critical of those who used Art Nouveau motifs to ornament basic structures. His métro stations in Paris (1899–1904) are perfect examples of his principles: organic forms, structural honesty, the decorative element—the expression of sentiment is an integral part of the composition.

Baron Victor HORTA's (1861–1947) Maison du Peuple in Brussels (1896) is important both in terms of its construction and as a new building type. It was one of a series of "people's buildings," run by workers' cooperatives, which were introduced in 1894 after the new Socialist party gained seats in Parliament for the first time. The plan followed the contours of the site, and an ingenious section, which included a double staircase, contained all the supporting service spaces. Smaller rooms at lower levels supported the large, light, and airy space of the main meeting hall which rose three stories above the third-floor level. Inside the meeting hall the floor sloped, the roof undulated, and cantilevered balconies leaned over from inclined walls.

Curvilinear emphasis

The Art Nouveau interior of Baron Horta's private house in Brussels is one of the earliest of the genre. The innovative Horta later became a Classicist.

Fin de Siècle

Literally "the end of a century." The end of the nineteenth century, to be precise, but in reality a historical expression so loaded with meanings that a definition is virtually impossible. Use *fin de siècle* to describe the paintings of Edvard Munch (Norwegian, 1863–1944) or Gustav Klimt (Hungarian, 1862–1918) or movements like German Expressionism, and you're dead right. To talk of anxiety, of androgyny, of anarchy, of Richard Wagner (German, 1813–83) or Oscar Wilde (Irish, 1854–1900), will stir things up. The start? The 1890s. The end? 4 August 1914, when turning back became a forlorn hope.

1869 The Suez Canal is opened, halving the time of the journey from Britain to India. The engineer is the French Ferdinand de Lesseps.

1873 Cable cars (the world's first streetcars) are introduced in the streets of San Francisco.

1884 Cocaine, before its addictive properties are recognized, is used for the first local anesthetic—for an eye operation.

1875~1910
The Last of the Big Masonry Towers
United States of America

Roman inspiration— the Pantheon.

Henry Hobson RICHARDSON (1838–86) is credited with bringing to an end America's continuing uncritical reproduction of miscellaneous European styles (Neo-Greek, Neo-Palladian, etc.) and inspiring an original American style that was to lead to the development of the skyscraper. His buildings are massive and solid, with simple strong forms that give a feeling of robustness and reliability. Some critics referred to his work as "masculine" in appearance.

Richardson studied in Paris at the École des Beaux-Arts (1859–62) and then worked in the atelier of Henri Labrouste. He built some private houses that appear forward-looking in both an original use of material and irregular forms. His real influence is through his commercial buildings—down-to-earth, functional places such as railroad stations, warehouses, and libraries.

The Marshall Field Wholesale Building in Chicago (1885) is the most important of these buildings. Seven stories high, it did not make full use of the latest steel-frame technology but was instead constructed of solid, richly textured, load-bearing masonry with wide, arched openings. There was an absence of any applied surface decoration and an uncompromising clarity of line that was typical of the new rationalist approach.

AMERICAN REVIVAL

While the influence of the originality and rationality of Richardson's work can be clearly seen in the development of the work of the Chicago School and in emerging Modernism, his work was also the starting point for the very different approach of the revivalists of American colonial architecture, best represented by the practice of *Charles McKIM* (1847–1909), *William MEAD* (1846–1928), and *Stanford WHITE* (1853–1906). Their work follows Beaux Arts symmetrical planning but is much

Blackboard Jungle

Henri Labrouste (1801–75) was unusual in his time. As a student, he caused consternation among his masters with his reconstructions of antiquity that dared to suggest that those sparkling white stone buildings had actually been painted in garish colors, and used not for religious purpose but for more utilitarian, vulgar activities. His St. Geneviève Library was one of the earliest public buildings to use exposed cast-iron structures, shocking his contemporaries, wh[o] considered the materic[l] most unsuitable.

1895 The first moving pictures screened in Paris by the Lumière brothers. It is a gripping movie of workers leaving a factory. The cinema is born.

1896 Adolf Loos settles in Vienna, where he meets the Secessionist painters They do not get on.

1898 The Paris Métro, linking the city via underground railroad lines, is opened.

more adventurous, drawing on a whole variety of different European precedents —Moorish towers from Spain and the Pantheon or Roman baths—depending on the use of the building. The practice produced an enormous number of important public buildings, including the Boston Public Library (1887), with a façade copied almost directly from Labrouste's St. Geneviève Library in Paris. In New York City their masterpiece, the Pennsylvania Railroad Station (1904, demolished 1963), was both a spectacular monument to the success of the railroad company and a utilitarian service. Esthetically, it combined both the excitement of the future, with its innovative steel and glass roof over the concourse, and the reassurance of the past, with its heavy masonry façade based on the ancient Roman baths of Caracalla.

NAMES ON THE WALL

Architectural passions: **H. H. Richardson** *influenced both* **Stanford White** *of McKim, Mead, and White and* **J. W. Root** *of Burnham and Root. Both Richardson and White are described in biographies as "bon vivants," with White mysteriously described as "exuberant in other ways as well."* **Daniel Burnham** *is quoted as saying: "Make no little plans; they have no magic to stir men's blood." While his team built skyscrapers and the others built domestic architecture and public buildings, White must have made some BIG plans: he was shot dead at a theater rehearsal in 1906.*

Boston Public Library by McKim, Mead, and White (1887–93) is a restrained, academic design, copied from Labrouste's of St. Geneviève Library in Paris.

1866 Alfred Nobel (of Nobel Prize fame) invents dynamite. From now on unwanted buildings can be destroyed at a stroke.

1870 Chicago, with its population of 300,000, is now by far the largest city in the American West.

1884 Lewis Edson Waterman patents the eponymous fountain pen.

Waterman

1875~1910
Chicago, Chicago
High-Rise Heaven

Soon after the destruction of the great fire of 1871 and the period of depression that followed, Chicago was expanding again. Building development was rapid, and as space became more difficult to find and land values rose, pressure increased to fulfil the demands of commerce for yet more space. Taller buildings were the inevitable result.

The common element in this group of commercial buildings is the use of a new and radical invention—a steel skeleton structure—and, more importantly, the expression of this structure on the exterior of the buildings. These first "skyscrapers."

Originally the building had a projecting cornice

Louis Sullivan's Schlesinger-Mayer Store (now Carson Pirie Scott and Co.), Chicago (1899–1904), has white terracotta panels that follow the steel structure.

Emphasis of horizontal lines

as they were soon to be known, were still perhaps only 15 stories high, and it was to be nearly another 30 years before the real competition to build higher still started in earnest, and the next wave of tall buildings was to appear.

Louis SULLIVAN (1856–1924) is the most important of the designers. Credited as the originator of the phrase "form follows function," he was convinced that a logical starting point was a necessity for art. Early examples of his work are the Wainwright Building in St. Louis (1890) and the Guaranty Building in Buffalo (1894/5). In both of these buildings, while the steel structure itself is not actually visible, the rhythm of the framed construction and organization of the spaces within are expressed on the exterior of the

Going Up!
Iron and steel framing was a useful, all-around medium, brilliantly adapted in Britain during the railroad boom, and eventually imitated and extended in France and the U.S ...but not without a struggle with the stone loving purists. New York's Haughwout Building was complete in 1857, becoming th first iron-framed multi-story structure to be served by one of Elisha Graves Otis's (1811–61) passenge elevators. Hard to believe these were tested only in 1854. Otis's vertical spring-loaded ratchets soon faced stiff competition from abroad, but without his completely reliable product, the skyscraper would have been positively earthbound for years.

1890 At Wounded Knee 350 Sioux are massacred and the wiping out of Native Americans is almost complete.

1891 Published novels include *Tess of the D'Urbervilles* by Thomas Hardy (1840–1928), and *The Picture of Dorian Gray*, by Oscar Wilde (1854–1900).

1897 America's John Philip Sousa writes the ever-popular "Stars and Stripes Forever" Marine band march.

NAMES ON THE WALL

Half a dozen stories up, pollution and wind make opening windows a bad idea. A solution was arrived at by **Dr. Willis Haviland Carrier,** *who had to control temperature and humidity in a Brooklyn printing works. His rival,* **Stuart W. Cramer,** *patented a system in 1906 and coined the term "air conditioning." The Carrier Corporation continued to refer to their system as "manmade weather" until 1933. Their 1938 Conduit Weathermaster enabled the later development of open-plan offices, a feature of the 1950s.*

edifice. The composition of the façades still refers to the past: a Classical image with a rusticated base at street level and an attic housing industrial equipment. The façades are constructed in load-bearing masonry with a decorated frieze that includes bull's-eye windows and a projecting cornice.

The Reliance Building (1895) by *David BURNHAM* (1845–1912) and *John ROOT* (1850–91) is the earliest example of the fully fledged steel-frame tall building that is not then dressed up in masonry clothing. The base and attic are now barely visible as the middle zone of the cellular structure of the offices, the

soaring vertical framing, and the horizontal floor slabs are fully expressed. The most accomplished, however, is Sullivan's Carson Pirie Scott Store (1899-1904), where the rigorous expression of the new technology is finally achieved in a style that, for the first time, is completely independent from the past. Sullivan's use of surface decoration is sometimes considered contradictory to this rational approach, although he employs only contemporary Art Nouveau stylization of natural forms of plants and flowers—an abstraction that can be compared to the spatial abstraction of his façades.

Burnham and Root's best-known building, and possibly the most popular skyscraper, is the Flatiron in New York City, the tallest building in the world at the time of its construction in 1902. On a very prominent and dramatic site at the triangular intersection of Broadway and Fifth Avenue, it has all the recognizable characteristics of the Chicago School. It is 21 stories high, with the latest steel framing system but clad more conservatively with limestone and terracotta.

Burnham and Root took Chicago School buildings to New York with the Flatiron Building of 1902.

1883 Robert Louis Stevenson (1850–94) writes *Treasure Island,* the ultimate ripping yarn.

1888 James Keir Hardie (1856–1915) founds the Scottish Labour Party; in the same year, he suffers electoral defeat at Mid Lanark as the first Labour candidate .

1901 Hubert Cecil Booth (1871–1955) invents that wonderful machine, the vacuum cleaner.

1890~1920

Art Nouveau in Caledonia
Mackintosh

Mackintosh built the west wing of the Glasgow School of Art, housing the library, in 1907–9.

Solid, square, severe, and austere; oriel windows, massive chimneys, and battered walls. Charles Rennie MACKINTOSH'S *(1868–1928) work has similar characteristics to that of the Secessionists in Austria, where it was exhibited in 1900. Through the art magazine* The Studio *(1893) Mackintosh became an inspiration to Josef Hoffmann and other Art Nouveau exponents in Europe.*

Some You Win, Some You Lose

Mackintosh had the unique distinction of being better known in Europe than on his own turf. His work was not well received in Britain but the Austrian Secessionists lapped it up. Though he became a partner in the firm of Honeyman and Keppie (1904), Mackintosh seems to have had a problem with humans: his work was great but he couldn't handle people. He dumped architecture (1913) and devoted his time to painting, living in various British and continental locations. He never looked back, never got rich, and died at a young age. Ain't life a bitch?

The characteristics of the evolving "modern" style in Europe are also typical of the Scottish Tower houses, the subject of a paper given by Mackintosh to the Glasgow Architectural Association on

Call me Mr. Plain.
Mackintosh Furniture

Charles Rennie Mackintosh's furniture was delicate in all its phases, even at its trademark whitest. Though his early work used ornamentation on that famous pure white ground, as time went by his style became less fussy. Though the idea of "purity" is something associated with later periods of art and design, Mackintosh led the pack by a long shot in this respect, largely because of his ideas of proportion: geometrical in his famous Glasgow School of Art, elongated and purely wooden, and—in certain commissions what one critic called antipretty. This might have been promising had Mackintosh not thrown in the towel. But there you go.

Scottish baronial architecture—a vernacular type much sketched by Mackintosh. This was a rational style with massive stone walls that were structural, insulating, and defensive against high winds, with small windows to prevent excessive heat loss, and steeply pitched roofs and overhanging eaves to deal with wet and snowy weather. Mackintosh's forms, evocative of dramatic climate and wild, uncultivated landscapes, together with his delicate graphics, were perceived by exponents of Art Nouveau as a part of their organic and naturalistic tendency—allied to the Arts and Crafts Movement rather than to any modernist or industrial approach.

1904 Scottish dramatist James Matthew Barrie (1860–1937) writes *Peter Pan*. A statue of the eponymous lost boy is put up in London's Kensington Gardens eight years later.

1907 William Thomson, first Baron Kelvin, dies. A brilliant mathematician and physicist, he had put forward the concept of absolute zero (a state in which there is no energy in a gas, liquid, or solid). The Kelvin scale of absolute temperature was named after him.

1915 John Buchan (1875–1940) writes the spy thriller *The 39 Steps*, featuring the intrepid Richard Hannay dicing with death amid the banks and braes of Scotland.

I BELONG TO GLASGOW

Mackintosh designed interiors for many Glasgow tea rooms, the fashionable, airy alternative to the dark and smoke-filled pubs. The Buchanan Street tea room (1897) was stenciled with elongated figures reminiscent of the work of Klimt.

Mackintosh's work combines the rationalist ideas of construction with individual artistic expression. Space is given priority for the first time. At Hill House (1903) in Helensburgh, the importance of the design

The curving glass and metalwork in the Willow Tea Rooms, Sauciehall Street (1904), typify Mackintosh's elegant interior work in Glasgow.

of the interior space can be seen clearly —the spaces appear as carved out from the inside, and great care is taken over the relationships between rooms and views out across the landscape. Rather than the form of the building dictating the space inside (Neoclassical), the exterior form is a result of the process of internal spatial composition (modern).

Mackintosh won the contract to design his best-known and mostaccomplished work, the Glasgow School of Art, in 1896. The handling of the complex relationship between internal spaces and volumes and the exterior form, the control of the daylighting, and the building's relationship to the site, set it apart from any other construction of this date.

NAMES ON THE WALL

Francis Newberry *(director, Glasgow School of Art) brought* **Mackintosh**, **Herbert McNair**, *and* **Frances** *and* **Margaret MacDonald** *together because he had noticed a similarity in their work. As "The Four" they exhibited at the Arts and Crafts Exhibition Society's exhibition in 1896, where the reputation for weirdness of the influential* **Beardsley–Wilde** *circle appeared to have rubbed off on them, earning them another name, "The Spooks." A journalist writing in 1897 had to reassure readers that the sisters were "cheerful, healthy girls," showing no sign of morbid obsession.*

1895 The first-ever X ray is taken, showing the ringed hand of Bertha Roentgen. Her husband, Wilhelm, has discovered electromagnetic radiation.

1898 The Finnish composer Sibelius, funded by the Finnish state, begins to write the first of his nine symphonies.

1899 Ernst Ludwig, Grand Duke of Hesse, admires Olbrich's Secession Building for the new group of artists so much that he brings him to Darmstadt to found an artists' colony where artists can build their own houses.

1840~1920

Getting Away from It All
Secession

Joseph Maria Olbrich designed the revolutionary Secession Building, Vienna (1897–98) as an exhibition ho for the works of the progressive painters the day. The building made his reputatio

"Nothing that is not practical can be beautiful" was the uncompromising statement of Austria's most progressive architect, Otto Wagner (1841–1918), at the end of the nineteenth century. In his inaugural lecture, at the Imperial Academy of Art in Vienna in 1894 (subsequently published as Moderne Architektur*),*

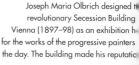

he also called for an end to the continuing reworking of eighteenth- and nineteenth-century "styles" and demanded that a young generation of architects develop a new architecture. They must reject the past, reject historicism, and look for inspiration to "modern life" and "the new requirements of our time."

W agner started out working in a clearly Neoclassical style and continued in the Art Nouveau style in the train stations he designed for the Vienna Stadtbahn (1894–1901). He achieved a level of success that earned him the commission to replan the city of Vienna and an appointment to teach at the Academy. In his later work we can see a clearer demonstration of his principles. Rather than the use of the symmetrical compositions of Neoclassicism, together with its extensive vocabulary of carvings and molding to decorate the façades that cover and conceal the structures beneath, we start to see the different building materials exposed for the first time. We are invited to see that the materials of both the walls and floors and of waterproofing and structure can be considered part of the sensual experience of a building.

Otto Wagner's most important building is the Post Office Savings Bank in Vienna (1906).

SPOT THE STYLE

Architects of the Vienn Secessionist group we looking to develop a sty that was not copied fro historical precedent. Usefulness was their starting point. Building had to be practical, which led them to develop distinctive façades using glazed tiles, ceramics, and sto cladding panels, whic could be easily washe down and would not discolor as brick and stone buildings did in tl soot and grime of turn of-the-century-cities.

1899 Such is the headache caused by the confusion of styles and ideas in the art world that the German firm Bayer A. G. markets the first aspirin tablets to help everyone cope.

1900 Freud's *Interpretaton of Dreams*, based on his clinical work in Vienna, is first published, and shocks everyone.

1919 In Russia, revolution holds sway. In Britain, Lady Astor becomes the first female Member of Parliament.

The Studio

This art journal exerted a powerful influence over design practice at this time—for instance, bringing Mackintosh's work to the attention of Austrian architects. M. H. Baillie Scott was introduced to medieval furnishings through its illustration of a Burne-Jones tapestry; the Grand Duke of Hesse discovered Baillie Scott's work through *The Studio* and commissioned him to work on the Palace of Darmstadt.

The exterior cladding is of marble slabs fixed visibly with aluminum bolts; inside, a glazed barrel-vaulted roof covers the main hall. An effortless elegance is achieved with a simple, straightforward, and efficient design.

Among Wagner's most well-known pupils are the Vienna Secessionists *Joseph Maria OLBRICH* (1867– 1908) and *Josef HOFFMANN* (1870–1956). The work of the group is characterized by use of cubic forms and attention to the quality of materials, though there is still an affinity with the Art Nouveau of France and Belgium. The Secession Building by Olbrich established his reputation and

Otto Wagner's church of St. Leopold (1904–7), known as "am Steinhof," has façades clad with marble slabs visibly fixed with aluminum bolts.

demonstrated the new approach. The form is of a square and solid base, of smooth, uncluttered surfaces, and the roof sports a hemispherical dome of filigree metalwork—a combination of both the rationalist construction and stylized organic decoration of Art Nouveau.

1879 Edison perfects the electric lightbulb and a crowd of 3,000 people gather on New Year's Eve for the first display of public streetlighting. The modern world is taking off.

1905–6 In Chicago, the first public building in reinforced concrete is constructed, by Frank Lloyd Wright himself —Unity Temple, in Oak Park.

1910 Frenchman Georges Claude develops neon light, and advertising signs are set to be part of city buildings.

1900~1940

So Long, Frank Lloyd Wright
An American Genius

New York's Guggenheim Museum (begun 1946, completed 1959) is famous for its curving profile and interior spiral ramp.

The Arts and Crafts Movement had declined in England by 1900 but continued in Germany and in the U.S. for another 20 years. Frank Lloyd WRIGHT (1867–1959), one of America's most famous architects, was a founding member of the Chicago Arts and Crafts Society, which was set up in 1897. He worked for Louis Sullivan before starting in independent practice. An unlikely American hero, Wright had a reputation for being arrogant and difficult with clients, colleagues, and assistants.

Wright's early buildings were large suburban houses. In contrast to European architects exploring ideas of minimum housing and inexpensive workers' housing, Wright's houses are luxurious. The Prairie Style houses, as they are known, have a distinctly horizontal character—long and low. They are open plan, with big fireplaces, and have shallow pitched roofs and overhanging eaves. The Robie House (1909) in Chicago is the last of the series.

Falling Water, Pennsylvania (1936–37), has a sloping woodland site with a river running through it.

1914–18 The First World War devastates France, Belgium and the lowlands of northwest Europe. The human cost is tremendous; the war decimates the male population of the countries that were involved.

1943 Albert Hoffman discovers the hallucinogen LSD.

1957 The first "manned" journey into space is made by a Russian dog, Laika, in the spacecraft *Sputnik II*.

INTERNATIONAL SCENE

Wright's early work in the Arts and Crafts style was of interest to European architects, notably the Dutch such as *Hendrik Berlage* (1856–1934). By the 1930s Wright's work was seen as part of the International Style, both in form and material innovation. Falling Water, the house in Bear Run, Pennsylvania (1936–37), is a composition of cantilevered concrete slabs; the Johnson Wax administration building in Racine, Wisconsin (1936–39), is built with the recently developed reinforced concrete mushroom columns.

NEW YORK CITY

Wright's most interesting building, unlike anything earlier, is the Solomon R. Guggenheim Museum in New York City. Wright's expressionistic form has a direct relationship with the interior. An inverted conical spiraling ramp wraps itself around an open atrium. The continuously sloping floor and the continuously curved vertical wall makes visitors self-aware: there is no static space in the museum, the perception is one of continuous movement.

A Busy Life

Wright led an extraordinary life. He was Sullivan's most important pupil, anticipated many of Le Corbusier's ideas, and influenced the Dutch De Stijl movement as well as Walter Gropius. He sympathized with much Arts and Crafts thinking but wrote *The Art and Craft of the Machine* to challenge William Morris's aversion to technology. He lived until age 90 and was married four times.

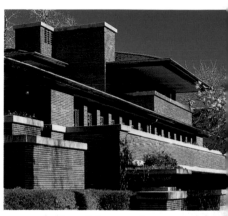

The influential Robie House, Chicago (1909) marks the climax of Wright's Prairie Style houses, which have terraces merging into gardens, projecting roofs, and rooms running into one another.

NAMES ON THE WALL

Of all the countries in Europe, Holland, especially the expressionist Amsterdam School, was most receptive to Frank Lloyd Wright's architecture. Work by **Jan Wils** *and* **Rob van t'Hoff** *directly reflects his influence, while established architects like* **H. P. Berlage** *(1856–1934) and De Stijl activists like* **J. J. P. Oud** *(1890–1963) were keen to spread the Wrightian message. Wright's designs appeared in* Wendingen, *the journal of the Amsterdam School and their 1925 special edition was regarded by Wright as the best monograph of his work.*

1916 Giorgio de Chirico (1888–1978) produces a typical painting—*The Disquieting Muses*—with dreamlike distortions of Classical building elements.

1915–18 Carl Jung and Alfred Adler defect from under Freud's "umbrella," believing there is more to life than sex.

1921 Luigi Pirandello's new play, *Six Characters in Search of an Author*, is performed. No one knows who is who and what is what.

1909~1919

Faster, Faster
Italian Futurism

There is little built work to exemplify the Futurist Movement. Architecture is represented principally by hundreds of drawings by the Italian architects Antonio SANT'ELIA *(1888–1916) and his friend Mario* CHIATTONE *(1891–1957).*

Speed was the obsession of the Futurists.

Like many other architects of their generation across Europe, they were fascinated by the possibilities offered by new technologies, and were ready to reject the past in favor of a radical new architecture. Their drawings show perspectives of a world unknown at the beginning of the century—cities on a massive scale with multilevel roadways and ziggurat forms leading to slender towers pointing toward the sky. The images have a romantic quality; they present a Utopian vision that has persuaded many architects since that the world of new technology, of high-speed circulation, and new metropolitan landscapes can be exciting.

MANIFESTOS

The Futurist Movement, which included artists from different disciplines, was led by *Filippo Tommaso* MARINETTI (1876–1944). The first manifesto was published in 1909, in the *Figaro* newspaper in Paris. It stated, "We affirm that the world's magnificence has been enriched by a new beauty: the beauty of speed." Further manifestos elaborated on an uncompromising call for a complete break with the past and the need to find expression for society's new concern—speed. Architecture was established in the manifesto with a contribution from Sant'Elia in 1914, following an exhibition of his work with the Nuove Tendenze group of artists in Milan. The "Messaggio" of Nuove Tendenze called for an architecture that rejected ornament and historicist form "where we see the lightness and proud

Futurismo e Fascismo

Futurism is one of the most fascinating areas in twentieth-century art and architecture. It comprised desire for artistic change combined with a large slice of real anarchy, plus a declared need to "cleanse" one's own society. It's all bombast but too close to our own time for comfort. Architecture was, like film, comparatively low on the Futurist agenda. But from where we stand, even though none of Sant'Elia's castles in the air were ever built, his scheme for "The New City" (La Città Nuova) is a foretaste of Fritz Lang's movie *Metropolis*, itself a prototype of Ridley Scott's *Blade Runner*. Pre-1914 Futurismo did not make it to the Armistice, but its chief polemicist, Marinetti, did, with nearly every other involved artist. Their varying associations with Mussolini and Fascism were a combination of bad news and bathos.

1922 James Joyce's *Ulysses* is published. Consciousness streams.

1927 Al Jolson's golden voice is heard in *The Jazz Singer*, the movie that ushers in the talkies.

1932 In the United States 16 million people are unemployed. They and their dependents represent about a quarter of the nation.

NAMES ON THE WALL

The Futurists were the punk rockers of the early part of the century: provocative performance artists who issued manifestos on a vast range of subjects, including one on smells. Although not many objects were produced, there were few aspects of design, or indeed contemporary life, on which the Futurists didn't have a policy. **Giacomo Balla's** *writing on 'Antineutral Clothing' called for garments that could be dynamic, aggressive, amazing, phosphorescent, and decorated with electric lightbulbs.*

The most detailed of Sant'Elia's drawings of La Città Nuova, 1914. The skyscrapers, high-density, and high-level circulation have all become part of town planning.

slenderness of girders, the slightness of reinforced concrete … aping the solidity of marble," which instead should be meaningful and refined, inspired by the world of machines, new technologies, and new materials.

INFLUENCES

Sant'Elia and the sculptor Boccioni (1882—1916) were both killed in 1916, and it seems that Futurism died with them. No further Futurist works were produced, and exhibitions that followed continued to show the same drawings. Nevertheless, Futurism and the principles it expounded have been of enormous influence. Its formal influence has been traced through Constructivism and the rational architecture of the modern movement, but, more importantly, it is the basis for a technological determinism expounded by such innovators as Buckminster Fuller, Renzo Piano, and the avant-garde English group Archigram.

Rationalism

A modern program, based on Futurism, was set up in Italy in 1926 by Gruppo 7. The most important member was Giuseppe Terragni (1904–43), who founded it together with Luigi Figini (1903–84), Gino Pollini (1903–), and Marcello Piacentini (1881–1960). Notable buildings are Olivetti's headquarters at Ivrea (1948–50), and the Church of Madonna dei Poveri in Milan (1952–56).
Terragni built the Casa del Fascio (local Fascist party headquarters) in 1932–36. Allied to Fascism, the movement was short-lived. The overbearing monumentality of the buildings for the 1942 Expo, EUR Rome, are a bleak reminder.

1908 Henry Ford devises the assembly line for the mass production of motor cars. Working on the line is here to stay, and where do art or craft fit in?

1908 A meteor collides with a herd of reindeer and devastates part of central Siberia, proving that the machine can't solve everything.

1913 Stravinsky's *Rite of Spring* is performed for the first time, by the Diaghilev Company, in the newly built Champs-Élysees Theater, Paris.

1907~1939

Deutscher Werkbund
The Age of Concrete and Glass

The Deutscher Werkbund (German Work Union) was set up in 1907 by a group of like-minded architects,

For Peter Behrens, the Age of the Machine needed good, honest buildings for its industries. The AEG Turbine Factory in Berlin (1909) is an early example of an industrial esthetic.

artists, and industrialists. Architect members, who included Peter BEHRENS (1868–1940), Walter GROPIUS (1883–1969), and Bruno TAUT (1880–1938), shared William Morris's disdain for the shoddy nature of mass-produced goods and materials. However, unlike the Arts and Crafts movement, they accepted industrialization as necessary to progress. So they set out to improve standards through cooperation with industrialists by means of education and design developments.

Crystal Clear

Together with concrete the exciting new material at the beginning of the twentieth century was glass. The most obvious development was fully glazed walls. Developments in concrete framing systems that allowed floor slabs to be cantilevered also allowed façades to be free of the structure. They could become lighter and more transparent. The experience of the spaces created by such large areas of glazing was also very different, affecting daylight and shadow and the endless possibilities of vistas both inside and out.

There was no particular visual image: the new objects and buildings would evolve out of the new methods of production, and the use of new materials and techniques. The Werkbund's annual publication included works from diverse fields of handicrafts, applied arts, graphic design, and painting, and they continued to promote art–industry cooperation. There was still nonetheless the conflict between the desire for handcrafted work and the affordability of mass production.

Bruno Taut

Bruno Taut conceived of a future architecture in Utopian Socialist terms, which became fused with a layer of mysticism. Only architecture, he believed, could reawaken the spiritual life of the people. He described his Glass Pavilion for the 1914 Cologne exhibition as a "mere exhibition building." But his application of color, light, and water created effects that Postmodernists would be proud of.

1916 The *Daily News* prints an interview with the president of the Arts and Crafts Exhibition Society under the heading "British Plan to Beat the Germans —The Jam-Pot Beautiful".

1917 While war is waged in Europe, the Bolsheviks seize power in Russia.

1919 Mussolini founds the Italian Fascist party and wearing black shirts and funny pants becomes a feature of Italian political life.

THROUGH THE LOOKING GLASS

The first Werkbund Exhibition, in 1914 in Cologne, included Bruno Taut's glass pavilion, which explored the unconventional use of a material that was to become the mainstay of the modern movement in architecture. Walter Gropius, with *Adolf MEYER* (1881–1929), designed the Werkbund administrative offices, which have staircases contained within curved glass towers that allow views into the whole height of the stairwell, and changing views to the outside.

Walter Gropius worked in Peter Behrens's office for several years before setting up on his own. With Adolf Meyer he designed the Fagus Factory at Alfeld an der Leine in 1911, a prototype of International Modernism.

Angle windows

Glass curtain walls

NAMES ON THE WALL

The 1914 Werkbund Exhibition was conceived as a tour de force for the body that had been inspired by the British Arts and Crafts guild revival and now boasted a vigorous membership of over a thousand, and an ambitious touring exhibition program. Yet the arguments that raged back and forth in its wake nearly finished it off! **Hermann Muthesius** *(author of* Das Englische Haus*) put forward ten propositions with the aim of clarifying the group's aims, and got ten counter-propositions back from the Belgian* **Henri van de Velde**. *The debate over standardization versus creativity survived the war and rumbled on into the 1950s.*

The interest in new materials and techniques led to an exploration of their potential for new forms and spaces. This "expressionism" resulted in distinctive and original buildings, often for industrial use, with no historical models. The architecture of Peter Behrens's AEG Turbine factory (1908–09) is an expression of the power of electricity. *Hans POELZIG's* (1869–1936) water tower and exhibition hall at Poznan (1910) is far removed from the regularity of Classicism and the picturesque quality of Gothic. The work is highly subjective, bold, and experimental.

The Jahrhunderthalle (1913) in Breslau (now Wroclaw, Poland), designed by *Max BERG* (1870–1947), is the most innovative, using reinforced concrete for its huge dome, 213 feet/65 meters in diameter.

1911 Sergei Diaghilev (1872–1929), establishes the Ballets Russes in France.

1916–19 A group of Hungarians who fled to Vienna after the Hungarian revolution failed publish the magazine MA *(Today)* dedicated to modern art and architecture.

1924 The death of Lenin creates a great building opportunity for Alexei Shchusev, creator of New Moscow. Lenin's mausoleum, a pyramidal composition topped with a pastiche Classical temple, is built.

1920~1935

House Reds
Russian Constructivism

Russian Constructivism embraced the ideas of industrial production wholeheartedly. The buildings and projects are machinelike: constructed from machine-made standard components, planned methodically according to use, and extended to include the new technological paraphernalia of signs, searchlights, projection screens, and radio antennae. The drawings also have a mechanistic feel, using block-printing techniques, in sharp contrast to the handcrafted watercolor drawings of contemporaries.

Tatlin's tower, designed in 1919 as a monument to the Third International but never built, was to span the Neva River and outdo the Eiffel Tower, with its spiraling openwork girders and revolving, suspended halls.

Welcome to the Machine

Architecture and industrial production only combined at the end of the nineteenth century, when theorists argued that Germany (yes, again) might begin to compete with the world market if their national products were of exceptional quality. But first their applied arts had to improve. The Deutscher Werkbund was the first step. Founded in 1907 in Munich, it was an association of artists, architects, manufacturers, and writers. It had great influence on early industrial design. In time the Werkbund's standpoint became obscured by the interests of others, including many of the De Stijl group, Le Corbusier, and then the Bauhaus itself, ultimate art-house of the early-twentieth century. Industry and design finally enter a new phase.

The tower built by *Vladimir TATLIN* (1885–1953) as a model for a proposed 1,000foot/300-meter building, is the most widely known Constructivist work. Its dynamic shape of a logarithmic, spiraling, canted conical web evokes a science-fiction-inspired excitement of intelligent machines, speed, and the potential energy of electricity. The various spaces were to be contained within three pure shapes, a cube, a pyramid, and a cylinder suspended within the structure. Each was to revolve at different speeds and at different intervals—a visible

1920–33 In the United States Prohibition fails to stop a lot of people from drinking and having a good time.

1921 The Soviet composer Sergei Prokofiev (1891–1955) composes the opera *The Love for Three Oranges*.

1925 Sergei Eisenstein's blockbuster Socialist movie *Battleship Potemkin* creates a cinematic stir.

demonstration of time through movement within the exposed structure. Unfortunately the building never saw the light of day. Tatlin started out as a painter, and was also highly regarded as a sculptor and theater designer, often working with found objects.

Konstantin MELNIKOV (1890–1974) was the first of the Russian Constructivists to achieve recognition when he built the Russian pavilion in Paris for the 1925 Exposition Internationale des Arts Décoratifs et Industriels Modernes. His projects demonstrate a highly individual, progressive approach. At the Rusakov Workers' Club (1927) in Moscow, the plan is triangular in shape with auditoriums at each of the three levels. The top auditorium is visible on the façade, divided into three solid forms forcefully thrusting out, cantilevered between the circulation areas, which rise vertically, clad with transparent glazing.

Hello Russia! Let's Get Real!

The Russian Revolution had a major effect on all branches of the visual arts, and the story is immensely complicated. However, it's safe to say that, of all the arts, graphic design and propaganda made the biggest strides. Artists like Malevich (1878–1935) and Tatlin (1885–1953) and even Chagall (1887–1985) might have held center stage for a moment, with the general idea of showing the "harmony" in the new socialist order, but it didn't last. Lenin mistrusted culture as an avenue to the hearts of the people. Wriggle though they did, Russian artists and architects found little sympathy in Communism from that point on.

BACK IN THE USSR

The new Socialism was developing patterns of new social structures and institutions, prompting architectural research on town planning and communal housing. Moisei Ginzberg's Narkomfin housing block in Moscow (1929) has shared spaces and different-sized apartments, a style to be taken up later by the Modernists. The most radical town planner was *Nicolai MILYUTIN* (1889–1942), who proposed a form of continuous linear development. New towns are organized in parallel narrow strips in a logical order to separate residential areas from industrial—railroad and industry, followed by green belt and highway, followed by housing and park adjacent to farmland. The linear development simply continued to grow as necessary along the lines of the rail and road, including any existing towns along its path.

NAMES ON THE WALL

Within the Constructivist movement, but in contrast to the rationalist approach, a second group more interested in the abstract ideas of painters such as **Kasimir Malevich** *and* **El Lissitsky** *was formed, led by the* **Vesnin** *brothers,* **Alexander, Victor,** *and* **Leonid.** *Their design for the Leningradskaya Pravda (1921) illustrates all the concerns of the group, incorporating the romantic machinelike esthetic with a sedate, rectilinear, almost abstract flat elevation.*

1915
El Lissitzky
brings Russian
Modernism to
the West.

1915 J. J. P. Oud (architect),
Theo van Doesburg (painter),
and Gerrit Rietveld (cabinet
maker) meet and discuss their
mutual regard for Cubism.

1920s Stravinsky,
Schoenberg, and Bartók
all take pains to shatter
the conventional
notions of harmony
and tonality in music.

1910~1920

Going Dutch
De Stijl

Matisse invented the
term "Cubism."

*Cubism in art, the new "way of
seeing," meant objects and spaces
could be represented without using
Renaissance perspective systems.
Science that gives us knowledge
and analysis of the elements means
we don't have to see them from one
viewpoint. In architecture the "modern" position is
an important beginning, separating visual elements
and ideas from conventional representation.*

In Holland, in reaction to the quaint sculptural and picturesque work of the Amsterdam School, the De Stijl movement was about objectivity. The use of naturalistic forms was rejected in favor of an abstract language composed of straight lines, primary colors and black, white, and gray. The paintings of Piet Mondrian, one of the founding members of the group, are universally recognizable. In architecture, lines and planes intersect, suggesting continuity of space rather than enclosing boundaries. Huis ter Heide in Utrecht (1916) by *Rob van t'Hoff* (1887–1979) clearly shows these ideas expressed with vertical glazing disappearing into the oversailing roof planes.

The most explicit architectural expression of De Stijl is a house in Utrecht built by *Gerrit Rietveld* (1888–1964) in 1924 in collaboration with the client, the interior designer Truus Schrader Schroeder. It sits on a plot of land at the end of a suburban terrace—a diminutive 3-D Mondrian painting, more like a piece of furniture than a habitable building. The materials used and the standards of workmanship employed are irrelevant to the work. Nothing is machine-finished, nothing is handcrafted, there are no mitered joints, no

1924 In America the first quick-frozen peas are available commercially, thanks to Mr. Clarence Birdseye. Even food becomes abstract.

1929 In the Soviet Union the dreams of the revolutionists are turning sour. Trotsky is sent into exile.

1931 The painters Piet Mondrian and Theo van Doesburg are among the founding members of the artists' group Abstraction-Creation, bent on working in an ahistorical, nonfigurative modern style.

NAMES ON THE WALL

In Hungary there was a similar literary and artistic movement also associated with Cubism through the periodicals Tett *(Action), 1915–16, and* Ma *(Today), 1916–21.* **Farkas Molnar's** *(1897–1945) Red Cube House (1921) was an early exploration of these new ideas. A Czech Cubist movement grew up around a publication,* Umeleky Mesicnik, *from 1911. Building types and plans showed no change, only the addition of jutting, angled decorative elements to the façades, like the fractured paintings of Braque or Picasso. Examples are* **Josef Chochol's** *(1880–1956) apartment building in Prague (1913).*

turned moldings, no skillful carvings. Everything is made specially for this house but it could have been made by you or me. There are no exotic materials, no warm stones, no polished marble, no rich brickwork or polished wood grain. All the surfaces are paint: the different colors of paint. Form is apparent but insubstantial. Each of the elevations, with a combination of projecting and receding planes and lines, appears frail and intangible. The architecture is the experience of the space.

The Schroeder House, Utrecht (1924)—planes of primary colors, endless space, and almost ephemeral forms.

De Stijl Movement

Theo VAN DOESBURG (1883–1931) was the spokesman for the De Stijl group of artists. Originally a painter, he wanted to expand two-dimensional paintings into something spatial. The basic theory of the group, the Neo-Plasticism of Mondrian, was based on mathematical theory to reduce 3-D volumes to 2-D plans, and was published in the first issue of their journal *De Stijl* in 1917. J.J.P. OUD (1890–1963) was an active member of the group and his Cafe de Unie in Rotterdam (1924/5) is pure De Stijl. Oud fell out with the purist principles of Van Doesburg and moved on to more straightforward modernism.

Rectangular shapes

Plain, painted surfaces

Projecting horizontal planes

1919 The first commercial airline service is put into operation between London and Paris.

1920s The Deutsche Mark collapses and buildings can't be built. This gives everyone more time to design them and formulate their theories.

1922-31 The Russian Constructivist painter, designer, typographer, and architect El Lissitsky is living in the West and communicating excitedly with both Bauhaus and the De Stijl people.

1919~1933

Our House Is a Very Very Very Bauhaus
Gropius and Co.

The Bauhaus, "House of Building," was named by Walter GROPIUS (1883–1969) in 1919, when he took over the directorship of the School of Arts and Crafts at Weimar. Gropius had succeeded one of the Werkbund pioneers, Henri VAN DE VELDE (1863–1957), and work produced by the school was clearly inspired by the ideas of William Morris. Over a short period, under the directorship of Gropius, and subsequently Hannes MEYER (1889–1954), the work coming from the school evolved from a nostalgic craft-based type to the "functional" clean lines now synonymous with the Bauhaus name.

Dramatically cantilevered balconies on Gropius's new school for the Bauhaus (1925–6).

The aim of the Bauhaus school was "to collect all artistic creativity into a unity, to reunite all artistic disciplines ... into a new architecture." In line with the changing methods of production, teaching methods were also changing. Work was carried out in teams, collectively, and in workshops rather than the traditional studios or ateliers led by "masters." There was also a common foundation course for students of all disciplines, basic courses in form, color, and materials, which were taught by artists including painters such as Paul Klee, Wassily Kandinsky, and Johannes Itten. Later, industrial design was taught to students.

NAMES ON THE WALL

During his time in England Gropius worked with **E. Maxwell Fry** *(1899–1987), famous for the pioneering Sun House, Hampstead, London (1934–35). Maxwell Fry was involved with the Modern Architecture Research Group (MARS), founded in 1933 alongside other Modernists such as* **Berthold Lubetkin, Wells Coates,** *and* **Ove Arup**. *They were interested in introducing European rationalist theories to England. Their most controversial project proposed reconstructing London on a linear plan.*

1924 Schoenberg produces 12-tone music. During a performance, the conductor stops the music and tells the audience not to hiss.

1926 In Britain a general strike rallies to support the miners, who have been locked out after disputing changes to working hours and pay.

1929–31 Le Corbusier builds his ultramodern Villa Savoye at Poissy.

THE LEADER OF THE GANG

Walter Gropius was the most important architect of the Bauhaus and one of the most important figures in twentieth-century architecture. He was commissioned to design the new buildings when the school moved to Dessau, and the workshop block is a model for Bauhaus modernism. It has mushroom columns supporting cantilevered concrete floor slabs; the spaces are enclosed by a three-story-high glass wall.

As well as his investigations into the uses of new materials—glass and concrete—Gropius was also involved with spatial and sociological aspects of developing modernism. His project for a Total Theater (1926) was exhibited in Paris in 1930 but was unfortunately never realized. The theater was to have had an interior space that could be modified as proscenium, circus, or amphitheater for different kinds of performance.

Gropius's housing projects evolved from a concern with the social needs of people living in ever denser urban areas. His apartment designs were evolved as a rational response to the need for fresh air, daylight, open spaces, and so on. The results at Siemenstadt (1929) are five-story blocks orientated north–south with planted parklike spaces between; this became the model for many similar projects to come.

The Architects' Collaborative

When the Nazis came to power in 1933, Gropius left Germany, as did many other Modernist architects. After a period in England, in 1937 Gropius went to the U.S. where he was Chair of the Department of Architecture at Harvard University. Still committed to the important idea of teamwork, he formed The Architects Collaborative, working alongside a group of much younger colleagues. They designed several notable buildings, including the Harvard Graduate Center (1950) and, after Gropius returned to Germany, the Berlin Interbau housing block (1957), with its dramatically curved balconied façade, set above an open ground floor.

Bauhaus

The design school par excellence, a Renaissance studio of the 1920s, and the only school in Europe teaching industrial design. At its height, the staff roster was like a roll-call of the very best in Modernism, including Johannes Itten (1888–1967), main mover and king of color theory, Paul Klee (1879–1940), Wassily Kandinsky (1866–1944), Marcel Breuer (1902–81), Josef Albers (1888–1976), and Lionel Feininger (1871–1956). Hannes Meyer intended to shift the school's emphasis away from estheticism to social issues, "the needs of the people instead of the needs of luxury."

The Graduate Center at Harvard University, Cambridge, Massachusetts, was built by Gropius and his associates in 1949–50.

1909 Charles-Édouard Jeanneret is working for Perret in Paris when Bakelite comes on the market—in the first commercial use of plastic, the synthetic polymer is used for electric plugs.

1928 By a happy accident, Alexander Fleming (1881–1955) discovers penicillin.

1929 The Wall Street crash ruins fortunes overnight as the stock market suddenly realizes it's all on paper.

1887~1965
The Sage
Le Corbusier 1

The Villa Savoye, Poissy, France (1928–30) has its main rooms on the first floor, which is raised on *pilotis* (those posts on the left).

Modernism was not just another style, a different esthetic; it rejected the whole notion of "styles" and proposed a new way of thinking. In a fast-moving modern society, architecture should be concerned with the machine culture: a culture of logic, of efficiency and purpose. Modern architecture has therefore evolved, at first tentatively, alongside developments in construction technologies and experiments into the uses of different materials.

Dom-ino House (1914–15)

Le CORBUSIER (*Charles Édouard JEANNERET*, 1887–1965) was an architect of exceptional brilliance. He worked for Behrens in Berlin and Auguste Perret in France, settling permanently in Paris. His early works have all the modern characteristics of the Bauhaus "style" of Gropius—white planes and cubic forms.

CIAM

European architects interested in the new architecture came together in 1928 to form CIAM (Congrès International d'Architecture Moderne). Its stated aim was "action to drag architecture from the academic impassé and to place it in its proper social and economic milieu." Originally intended as an informal gathering of creative individuals, it became enormously influential as a forum for discussion and dissemination of ideas and information. It continued for around 30 years, before a new generation of radicals, known as Team X, replaced it.

In 1923 he published *Vers une Architecture*, a strident manifesto for a new architecture that used examples of ocean liners, airplanes, and cars to support his arguments for logical design. Fundamental to the new architecture was the use of a framed structure, developed with vertical columns supporting horizontal floor slabs. Corbusier formalized the theory that evolved through a series of practical projects, naming it the "5 points." Columns (*pilotis*) on individual foundations raise the house above ground level; flat roofs can be used as roof gardens or terraces, as useful space and insulation; without the constraints of supporting the upper floors, walls can be anywhere, allowing a free (or open) plan; long windows stretch full length between the vertical columns, allowing daylight and fresh air to flood into the spaces; the free façade can be composed

1930 Amy Johnson flies solo from London to Australia, taking 19.5 days.

1947 The end of the Raj. India gains independence. Soon Le Corbusier will be working in Chandigarh.

1952 The malarial mosquito is at last pronounced extinguished in Ceylon (Sri Lanka) after a seven-year struggle with DDT.

Big Building

Le Corbusier developed a particular kind of formal composition for larger buildings. The Pavillon Suisse at the Cité Universitaire in Paris, the Cité de Refuge in Paris, and the Centrosoyus in Moscow all show similar ideas: small repetitive spaces, the bedrooms or offices arranged in an orderly fashion, stacked up in a slab block and carefully dimensioned to allow light to enter correctly. At ground level, spacious, curved, and independent shapes contain entrance lobbies and communal facilities. Circulation areas are used to articulate the main forms. The whole is a visible expression of what is contained within.

independent of main structure.

HOUSES

Villa Savoye (1928-30) and Maison La Roche (1923) are examples of a type that have become monuments to Modernism. Lofty double- or triple-height spaces would appear alongside more customary ceiling heights. Conventional corridors have been replaced with ramps, bridges, and galleries. Movement from one space to the next allows

A People Person

Le Corbusier's architectural and town planning schemes had people in mind from an early stage. In 1904 he met Tony Garnier (1869–1948), famous for his ideas for a Cité Industrielle, which were known to Le Corbusier circa 1904, published in 1917, and therefore predated Futurism by at least five years. Garnier's giant scheme involved the use of concrete and lots of glass. Le Corbusier married Garnier's ideas to the concept of human solitude within a larger living organism: the commune. In 1923 he published his views on a satisfactory partnership between form and the intellect in a book *Vers une Architecture* (Toward Architecture). His ideas for universal cities, with high-rises centrally and symmetrically located, are not dissimilar to those behind much new town planning today.

interaction with the main spaces of the house. All rooms are filled with daylight, and dramatic shafts of sunlight enter from carefully placed windows. Exterior spaces around the building are as much a part of the composition as the interior spaces, with outside views carefully framed. These "machines for living in" have the spatial richness and luxury Le Corbusier intended for all dwellings.

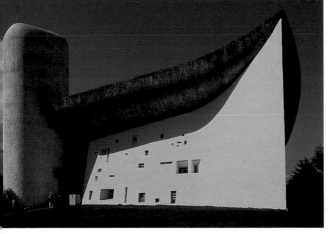

The church of Notre Dame-du-Haut, Ronchamp (1950–54), a much later work, shows the refinement of his ideas.

1914 Bruno Taut, who has Utopian views about modern architecture and is keen to use all the latest technology, designs the House of Glass for the Werkbund's Cologne exhibition.

1916 Einstein publishes his *Theory of General Relativity*, but during World War I no one takes much notice.

1916 In Zurich Hans Arp and Tristan Tzara form the antiart Dadaist movement.

Better Late than Never

In architecture the term expressionism exists in a kind of time-warp after its fine art predecessor. Architecture acknowledges the prewar frisson of this new tendency, but tends to reserve its applause for post-1918 wunderkinder. The semiabstractions of Art Nouveau are a kind of launchpad, from which flights of fancy take the curious around the creation of Antoni Gaudi (we meet him later), some nice Amsterdam housing estates, Copenhagen's Gruntvig Church (Klint, 1913–26), and thence to Mendelsohn' concrete with attitude.

1920~1960

Expressionism
Natural Generations

The architecture of the Werkbund at the beginning of the twentieth century is clearly linked to the development of Modernism—from Gropius and Meyer's model factory at Alfeld an der Leine and Gropius's move to the Bauhaus. However, not all architects followed this line. The Expressionist ideas of Bruno TAUT (1880–1938) and Hans POELZIG (1869–1936) presented an alternative to the easily adopted formalism that resulted in International Modernism, with its pure geometries and rational planning.

The interior of Berlin's concert hall, the Philharmonie (1956–63), shows Hans Scharoun's distinctive geometry.

Expressionism's icon is the Einstein Tower at Potsdam built by *Erich MENDELSOHN* (1887–1953) in 1920. The building is conceived as a sculptural object: a plastic and naturalistic form, curvaceous and unlike any pure geometrical shape. Mendelsohn was concerned about the polar

oppositions at the Werkbund. Noting the same division in Holland, he described the work of Berlage and Michel de Klerk in Amsterdam as "visionary but with no objectivity," and architecture by J. J. P. Oud in Rotterdam as "functional without sensibility." Neither extreme was satisfactory, and Mendelsohn worked to achieve a synthesis of both:

the rational and functional together with the expressive or dynamic. His 1921 Hat factory at Luckenwalde is highly articulated, having a long, low production area with undulating, multiple pitched roofs juxtaposed with a smooth-faced, tall, flat-roofed and angular cubic block. Mendelsohn's later work increasingly used pure geometries but retained characteristically confident: sweeping curves in plan, heavy powerful horizontals, and extensive glazing.

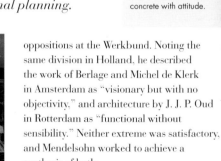

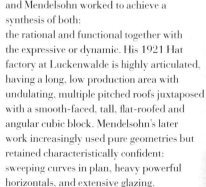

1918 In England women are at last given the vote, but they have to be over 30 to exercise it.

1915 Czech writer Franz Kafka's short story "The Metamorphosis" is published. Expressionism is in the zeitgeist.

THE UTOPIAN

As a young architect and a member of the "Glass Chain" (the group of 14 architects launched by Bruno Taut for the exchange of ideas), *Hans SCHAROUN* (1893–1972) produced some of the most enduring visionary sketches of the time —dreamlike images of a Utopian future. During the 1930s and 40s, Scharoun's work was limited to private houses. All show an originality of form and asymmetrical composition related to the specifics of a particular site.

In the 1950s and 60s, he had the opportunity to build a series of larger buildings. The Philharmonie and the National Library in Berlin are both enormously important, with an inventiveness and originality that remain individual to Scharoun. Neither conforms to any recognizable formal geometry or any type— the experiential quality is paramount.

Erich Mendelsohn's Einstein Tower at Potsdam (1920) has the sculptural quality of his early Expressionist work (much of which was on paper) in the years after World War I.

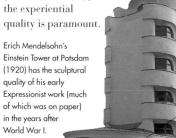

Curved forms —the new concrete esthetic

The importance of the individual, whether focusing on the orchestra or in the library looking at a book, is as much a part of the total architecture as the shared spaces of foyers and entrance halls.

Scharoun

During the Nazi period in the 1930s and 40s, Scharoun's work was limited to building private houses. These show a development of his ideas about architecture's relationship to the landscape, with carefully designed external spaces and gardens. He also produced a great deal of drawings during this period, ideas that would be used for later projects.

1928 Bubblegum makes its debut. Perhaps it helps Bucky Fuller to dream up his geodesic domes for chewing it in.

1932 Alvar Aalto invents curved plywood furniture, which comes in handy for his undulating Finnish Pavilion at the Paris Exhibition of 1937.

1957–58 Scientists of many nations get together to study the earth in International Geophysical Year.

1920~1970

Down with Geometry
Organic

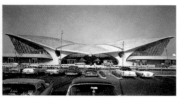

The TWA Terminal at Kennedy Airport, New York, by Eero Saarinen (1956–62), uses naturalistic forms that are suggestive of flight.

"Organic architecture" is a term loosely applied to anything that isn't composed of pure geometric forms, but looks as if it could be natural. Its roots are in the late nineteenth-century search by architects for an alternative to the endless copying of other styles. Nature offered a variety of forms as inspiration, particularly curves.

You don't find straig lines in nature.

As with Expressionist architecture, there is an emphasis on the specifics of climate and topography in determining relationship with the landscape. The idea of being "in harmony with nature" has been an important consideration for many Modernist architects—Sullivan, Aalto, and Scharoun, for example, though their approach is related to process (the evolution of form in response to a series of issues related to the brief, the site, and anticipated use) rather than a direct visual interpretation of "natural-looking" forms.

NATURAL HARMONY

For *Hugo Haring* (1882–1958), the natural world legitimized the concerns of architects like Mendelsohn about the apparent opposition of the rational and the allusive. Nature has room for both—efficient forms, such as the streamlined greyhound dog breed, as well as flamboyant and assertive stag antlers. Haring's Gerkau Farm (1924) has barns and buildings for animals laid out without reference to any geometry or symmetry.

Others discussed in this context are *Eero Saarinen* (1910–61), whose TWA terminal at New York's Kennedy Airport (1962), looks like a bird in flight, and *Jorn Utzon* (1918–) those Sydney Opera House (begun 1957), has shell-like forms.

Oooh—Those Wavy Lines!
Art Nouveau's wavy tendrils ensured that most experimental architecture was moving away from the rectilinear by 1906, ably assisted by developments in concrete and cantilevering, which allowed new art forms into building projects. For great concrete, Pier Luigi Nervi (1891–1979) is the best. His Ortobello airplane hangars (1936 onward) are merely indicative of the kind of rib vaulting the Romans would have died for, and his sports stadia, including that for the 1960 Rome Olympics ... well, *bella* is simply an inadequate term.

1959 The hovercraft is demonstrated. It can move over land or water.

1961 The Berlin Wall is constructed, dividing the city of Berlin between West and East Germany.

1962 New Wave cinema is hitting the screens. This year Antonioni's *L'Aventura* is released.

NAMES ON THE WALL

Hermann Finsterlin *(1887–1973)*
built nothing but was the creator of an influential architecture of fantasy. He wrote prolifically of a world of organic form in which man's frozen creative energies would be restimulated by the Universe. In 1919 he spotted a forthcoming exhibition in a newspaper used to wrap his sausages and was pleasantly surprised by the interest taken in his work. A special edition of the Expressionist periodical Wendingen *followed. His sketches seemed so far beyond realization that he gained respect as an abstract theorist.*

In the 1990s the term "organic" has become popular again. It has been used for the architecture of the Hungarian *Imre Makovec* (1935–), who achieved international recognition for his pavilion at the Seville Expo of 1992. Makovec's buildings are visually anthropomorphic, generally using timber in all its different applications. The nave inside the Farkaset Mortuary Chapel could be the ribcage of a huge animal; the entrance to the church at Siofok (1986–90) looks like the face of an inquisitive owl. All his buildings have rough timber shingles resembling crocodile skins or scaly fish. The forms, developed primarily through the roof, are supposedly symbolic of a primitive Hungarian culture; most look like upturned boats. His work has been criticized for colluding with the romanticized version of Hungary's past, promoted by the politics of the new capitalism in an attempt to eradicate International Modernism, with its Socialist overtones.

That's A Good Idea

The craving for weirdness in the late 1970s brought the crazy world of Bruce Goff (1904–82) to notice. His houses employ a range of different geometries and materials individually tailored to clients, who are included, rashly, in the design process. His inventive ways of looking at how we live have resulted in such oddities as the Dace House in Oklahoma, with vast cylindrical cupboards on the façades apparently for practical storage. Yeah, Bruce, thanks very much.

The great sails of the Sydney Opera House, designed by Jorn Utzon and completed in 1973.

Lounges overlook the harbor

Precast concrete ribs support the vaults

The vaults all have the same curvature

1919 Le Corbusier and the artist Amedée Ozenfant (1886–1966) publish the book *Purist Manifesto* after Cubism.

1928 John Logie Baird (1888–1946) invents a scanning device that will become the television— the eye in the corner of the room.

1939–45 World War II; blitzkrieg and bombing bring devastation to cities all over Europe; when the war is over there will be a pressing need for housing.

Housing Estates

English Garden Suburbs began to appear in London in the late 1870s, reaching their apotheosis in Hampstead Garden Suburb (begun by Unwin in 1906), where domestic and public planning blended harmoniously. Postwar slum-clearance projects seized the opportunity to build apartment buildings to rehouse the dispossessed, and Robert Matthew's horrible Roehampton Estate in London (1958) followed Corbusier closely. However, Roehampton showed how this idea could go wrong.

1920~1970

The Living Machine
Le Corbusier 2

Le Corbusier's Modulor.

LE CORBUSIER was very much involved with twentieth-century Modernism's greatest project—the provision of housing for everyone. A socially motivated project, it developed from the slum-clearance programs of overcrowded nineteenth-century cities, started in earnest after World War I, and became a pressing political issue after the bomb damage of World War II. It was also part of the changing aspect of architectural production. Modernism, within the context of mass production, meant less expensive and more efficient production of housing for all.

L e Corbusier's mass-housing projects pursued the same ideas as his individual houses in terms of the importance of space and light, and also re-examined the way we inhabit our homes in a changing society. The outcome of all his ideas was the Unité d'Habitation in Marseilles (1947–52): a suburban town of 1,800 inhabitants all within one building. The vast concrete building, which has been likened to an ocean liner by many critics, is raised up on giant *pilotis* to let the landscape continue underneath. It has a roof terrace that, like the deck of a ship, has vast funnellike chimneys and a pool for children. The apartments, on two levels (duplex), are ingeniously organized across

The Unités make optimum use of flat roofs for recreation space.

the width of the building to allow sun to enter both morning and evening. The Unité includes shops, hairdressers, laundry, and nursery—all the facilities normal to a small town, as well as the apartments. A successful "type," several more were built in France and Germany.

1947 Buckminster Fuller (1895–1983) invents the geodesic dome; 50,000 are built in the next 30 years.

1951 Mies van der Rohe designs Chicago's Lake Shore Drive apartment buildings, while Frank Lloyd Wright is putting the finishing touches to the Friedman House in Pleasantville, NY.

1953 Spray-can mechanism devised by Robert H. Abplanalp; it becomes very easy to apply graffiti to concrete walls.

NAMES ON THE WALL

It would be impossible to talk about improvements in housing provision without acknowledging the input of **Ebenezer Howard**, *a British office worker who conceived the notion of the planned garden city after a stay in the U.S., and swayed architectural opinion through the force of his convictions and his commonsense approach. Although Germany had paid tribute to the charms of the English house, there was a suspicion that it was progressing the garden city idea faster than we could. British Prime Minister* **Lloyd George** *sent a mission to investigate in 1919. The term has been absorbed by most other European languages. There are cité-jardins, Gartenstadten, and Cuidad-jardin out there in abundance.*

in the 1950s, where outdoor access spaces were grouped together to promote neighborliness.

Powell and Moya's Churchill Gardens in London (1947–60) include some particularly elegant examples of slab blocks. The apartments, in nine-story-high blocks, are accessed in pairs from independent stairways encased in glass, set at right angles to the main structure. The flat roofs have terraces in the corners, and circular forms and railings recall the "ship" esthetic of Corbusier's Unités.

Citrohan House

Le Corbusier saw designs for housing as part of designs for towns, and vice versa. The Citrohan House (1924) featured two load-bearing walls and a double-height living space with a double-height terrace outside. The unit could be used in a terrace of houses or as a duplex in a multistory block. The house was exhibited at the Paris Exhibition in 1925 as the Pavillon de l'Esprit Nouveau. It included a tree growing through the roof and an exhibition space.

BUILDING BLOCKS

Many other architects had the opportunity to design public housing schemes, and developed new patterns of dwelling in response to changing patterns in society. Sir *Denys LASDUN* (1914–) evolved a "cluster" block

Ocean-liner-style chimney

Play deck

The roofline of the Unité d'Habitation displays huge funnellike chimneys, and is an area for recreation.

1900–1913 Cubism, Fauvism, Futurism, and the beginnings of Expressionism are all flourishing in the world of European painting, while Impressionism and Synthesism are still on the go.

1913 Poet Guillaume Apollinaire (1880–1918) presides over the Surrealist movement, and is to be seen walking his pet lobster along the Paris boulevards.

1924 At its new headquarters in Dessau, under the directorship of Gropius, the Bauhaus concentrates purposefully on architecture and industrial design.

1918~1960

A Star Is Born
Mies van der Rohe

"I don't want to be interesting; I want to be good." Ludwig MIES VAN DER ROHE (1886–1969), quoted above, managed both. Building throughout the first half of the twentieth century in Europe and in the U.S., Mies was responsible for probably the most-fêted building of the Modern movement, the German Pavilion at the Barcelona Exhibition of 1929. His famous dictum "less is more" can be clearly seen in the severe outward simplicity of his buildings, which understates the elegance and the subtle proportions.

Bronze and marble facing   Heat-proof glass

New York's glass-wrapped Seagram Building (1954–58) by Ludwig Mies van der Rohe and Philip Johnson was a new architectural symbol when it was built.

The German Pavilion is a development of his earlier De Stijl work in its painterly approach to the use of detached planes and lines to articulate space and imply enclosure. It goes further, with its use of exquisite materials—marble, onyx, glass, steel—proof that architecture can have a vitality, a monumental quality through material presence. The building is small in scale, single-story, and forms a simple rectangle in plan. The horizontal plane of the roof slab is supported on a regular grid of columns with the walls appearing as if randomly placed as perfect entities, separate elements independent of the structure.

It Ain't What You Do...

It fell to Mies to direct the Bauhaus in its last incarnation, from 1930–33, during the transit from Dessau to Berlin. Though Mies was wonderfully pragmatic, effectively changing the Bauhaus into an architectural institution, waiving many educational requirements to keep the place going, he failed finally in the face of Nazi intransigence. They saw it as a hotbed of "cultural Bolshevism." Nevertheless, Mies was happy enough to enter competitions for Nazi architectural commissions, and solicited votes for the party, along with the conductor Furtwängler and the sculptor Barlach. When he finally did leave Germany for America it was for a well-paid job in Chicago: he didn't see himself as a political refugee, but simply as an architect who had to make a living. He did. While he was no Nazi supporter, he was most definitely an opportunist, and as such—both at the time, and with hindsight —a figure occasionally without principle.

1961 The Russian Yuri Gagarin becomes the first man to travel in space. He orbits the world just once at a height of 188 miles in a time of 90 minutes.

1963 President John F. Kennedy is shot and killed. Everyone over the age of 15 will forever remember where they were that day.

AIRBORNE

Two other buildings from a later period, The Farnsworth House, Plano, Illinois (1950), and the New National Gallery, Berlin (1962–68), demonstrate Mies's continuing commitment to the same ideas. The Farnsworth House takes the idea of the horizontal plane to its extreme. In this single-story building, the floor slab is raised on columns but just enough so that it appears to be floating. This effect of detachment, of complete separation from structure, is enhanced by the slabs being attached to the sides of the columns.

The gallery in Berlin has clear glass walls all around, allowing an uninterrupted view of the underside of the dominating roof slab, which seems to hover above the supporting columns. In contrast to the light, airy, spacious, open feeling of the ground level, the basement level contains a walled garden, an enclosed, secluded, and secret space.

Berlin's New National Gallery (1962–68) is a logical continuation of Mies's style, in which engineering and architecture work together: simple and elegant.

NAMES ON THE WALL

Three moments in a career: in 1927 **Mies van der Rohe** *organized the exhibition* Die Wohnung, *which showcased the best Modern movement thinking on the problem of social housing provision. In 1946 Knoll Associates began promoting furniture designs from leading Europeans. Mies granted production rights of his classic 1920s oeuvre to Knoll. In the same period skyscrapers became increasingly cost-effective and corporate clients rushed to invest. The gleaming glass towers conceived of as an embodiment of a social vision were finally built, but as monuments to capital.*

GLASS HOUSES

Mies eventually built his skyscrapers. The Seagram Building, New York (1954–58, with Philip C. Johnson) is an office tower of sheer bronze, raised above a wide plaza. The quality of the materials and perfection of the detailing is more powerful than any elaboration of form or decoration. The Lake Shore Drive apartments, Chicago (1950–51), are a successful application of the same ideas to residential development.

A Late Starter

Mies wasn't trained as an architect. He learned his skills from his father, who was a master mason, and apprenticed himself to a furniture designer, Bruno Paul, before working in the offices of the architect Peter Behrens. After a few years there, he worked on his own ommissions, which are mainly rather romantic and Neoclassical in style; it wasn't until the end of World War I that he became active in the Modern movement.

1953–54 In Britain the term "brutalism" is coined for the new concrete architecture where ducts and all are on show.

1954 John Cage introduces minimalism to music as his "4' 33'" ("Four Minutes, Thirty-three Seconds") silently hits the scene in the concert hall.

1954 In Britain, wartime food rationing comes to an end. People are free to indulge their culinary passions.

1930s
Tecton and After
Modernism in Britain

The development of Modernism in Britain is associated with the arrival of a number of influential European architects en route for the States. Gropius, Breuer, Chermayeff, and Mendelsohn all completed building projects during their brief sojourns in England before going to the US.

Simple, oval plan

Low wall changes height

The Penguin Pool (1935) at the Royal Zoological Society (London Zoo) was designed by Lubetkin and Lindsey Drake.

Berthold *Lubetkin* (1901–90), a Russian, settled in London in 1931 and was a founding member of Tecton, a group of architects dedicated to the development of Modernism. Tecton's best known work is the Penguin Pool at London Zoo. This project was an opportunity to apply scientific, analytical methods to design: the architecture could provide for actual needs rather than exist as a romanticized simulation of a natural habitat.

The resulting building is a paragon of Modernism. Thin, curving walls form an elliptical enclosure containing the pool, which is embellished with the sinuous curves of two interlocking spiraling ramps. The concrete was the thinnest seen at the time, and the completely unsupported ramps seem to defy gravity. The continuous curves of the ramps, steps, and pool mean there is uninterrupted activity as the penguins move around.

GOOD HEALTH

Tecton built several other extremely important Modern buildings. The Finsbury Health Centre, London (1938–39), used a mural and a series of architectural sketches to inform the public of the benefits of fresh air, daylight, and sunshine. The building itself, a crisp and white curving form with glass block walls, is thus symbolic of the new imperatives toward health and fitness current at the time.

1954–58 Pier Luigi Nervi is working on the design of the UNESCO building in Paris—all made of concrete.

1956 Britain introduces a Clean Air Act, after smog kills several thousand in one London winter.

1957 The USSR launches the first earth satellites, Sputnik I and Sputnik II. The first USA satellite, Explorer I, is launched in 1958.

Two notable London buildings in the functionalist Modernist style are the Daily Express building on Fleet Street (1933), by Ellis and Clark, and the Peter Jones department store in Sloane Square (1936), by Slater, Moberly, Reilly and Crabtree. The key icon of 1930s British Modernism is the De La Warr Pavilion at Bexhill-on-Sea by Mendelsohn and Chermayeff (1935), with its expressed horizontality and cubic shape articulated with curved glazed stairwells.

Only the more progressive of British architects adopted Modernism. Others were still steeped in the Neoclassical and neo-Gothic. Tecton's flats in Highgate, London—High Point I and II— follow all Le Corbusier's principles, but most housing built in the 1930s only picked up formal aspects such as geometric shapes and white walls. Art Deco sunbursts were common on gates and doors, but steeply pitched roofs, quirky gables, and cramped plans showed the favored Gothic inspiration.

The Festival of Britain

The Festival of Britain in 1951 involved a whole series of exhibitions and buildings to house them. One was the Royal Festival Hall, a truly modern building. The dark, enclosed space of the concert hall is raised up on columns in the center of the building, quite separate from the foyer spaces that continue all around and underneath. The RFH was the first in a whole series of buildings to house the arts on London's South Bank. Almost all are exceptionally good pieces, such as the Hayward Gallery (1964, by the LCC Architect's Department) and the National Theatre (1967–77) by Denys Lasdun, where foyer spaces mingle pleasantly with the banks of the Thames River. The same vocabulary based on ideals of early Modernism are also seen in Congress House (1953–60) by David du R. Aberdeen. Cleverly planned on a tight urban site, it has a central courtyard that allows light into the offices and meeting rooms. The floor of the courtyard is the glazed roof of the conference hall below.

Erich Mendelsohn and Serge Chermayeff must have shocked the town's residents with their design for the De La Warr Pavilion at Bexhill-on-Sea, Sussex.

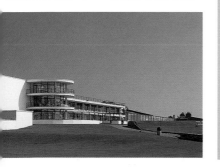

1917 When Aalto is 11 Finland gains independence from Russia.

1927 Oil is discovered in Iraq, leading to the development of the Middle East.

1948 The State of Israel is founded in Palestine.

1920~1960

The Northern Light
Aalto

Alvar AALTO'S *(1898–1976) recognition as part of the architectural avant-garde dates from 1929 after his work with Erik Bryggman on the Turku 700th anniversary exhibition and his participation in the CIAM meeting. The best example of his early work is the Paimio Sanatorium (1929), built in reinforced concrete, with flat white walls and strip windows. It has all the cool elegance of the best Modernist works.*

The intimately scaled civic center at Säynätsalo was built by Alvar Aalto in 1949–52 when the architect returned to Finland after working in the U.S.

Aalto's later works are visually very unusual. Like many other modern architects in the postwar period, he moved away from the International image of 1930s Modernism to investigate other materials and the specifics of location that tie a building to the landscape. He used timber and brick construction rather than the concrete and steel commonly associated with European Modernism. When Germany and France were developing a steel industry and precast concrete production, Finland with its vast natural timber sources developed the mass production of plywoods and laminated timber beams. The rules of Modernism rigorously applied allowed Aalto to develop projects in relation to the specifics of the geography, culture, and building traditions of his native Finland. Two pavilions, one for the 1937 Paris Exposition and one for

NAMES ON THE WALL

The most important Swedish architect is **Gunnar Erik Asplund** *(1885–1940). He designed Stockholm City Library (1920–28), Stockholm Exhibition Building (1930), and Göteborg Town Hall (1934–37).* **Sigurd Lewerentz** *(1885– 1975) developed a less "functional" and more poetic minimalism, seen in his churches at Skarpnack (1960) and Klippan (1963).* **Ralph Erskine** *(1914–) is famous for the Byker Wall public housing scheme in Newcastle (1969–75), which involved design consultation with the inhabitants.*

the 1939 New York World's Fair, raised Aalto's international profile, leading to a visiting professorship (1940–48) at the Massachusetts Institute of Technology. While there he designed Baker House

1956 Ingmar Bergman's film *The Seventh Seal* brings to cinema the classic Modernism of Scandinavian design.

1971 The pocket calculator now comes into use. The first model weighs a hefty 2.5 pounds.

1976 The space probes *Viking 1* and *Viking 2* investigate the possibility of life on Mars.

A Man of Many Talents

Aalto is as well known for his bent-plywood furniture (from 1932) as for his architecture. Why? Because he humanized it. No tubular Bauhaus steel here, thanks: only the real McCoy. And he kept the wood coming. A stacking three-legged stool that most of us couldn't put a name to is in regular use today, after its first appearance at the 1937 Paris Expo. Aalto's sensitivity is commonly noted, and commentators also point to the excellence of the work by his wife, Aino, which gets lost in the haze surrounding their joint distribution venture, Artek. In Alvar's architecture brick and timber mix coherently, with consistent understatement. Easy to forget and easy to accept, Aalto's work in architecture and design helped Scandinavian style to attain the position it enjoys today.

(1947) on the Charles River.

Two significant buildings from among Aalto's later works give a good illustration of his originality and individual approach. As part of his plan for Säynätsalo, a new town for 3,000 people, Aalto designed the town hall and library (1950). These comprised small-scale brick buildings, grouped around an open courtyard planted with grass, directly accessible, via wide steps, from the marketplace. The informal arrangement and small, almost domestic scale is a deliberate contrast to the idea of town hall as imposing monument. The architecture of Säynätsalo is not a symbol of the council's power, but a symbol of democracy, a truly public space.

The Vuoksenniska Church at Imatra (1952) has a clever plan with sliding partitions that allows the main nave space to be extended or reduced along its length to accommodate varying sizes of congregations. The main roof is divided into three vaults following these divisions, lifted above the surrounding solid walls to provide clerestory glazing. The entrance and other ancillary spaces are grouped at the side. The church has a tall slender tower close to the pine trees among which it stands.

The Paimio Sanatorium (1929–33) is one of many of Aalto's buildings of this period, which were to become classics of modern architecture.

Reinforced concrete

1912
Cellophane is
manufactured
and marketed
for the first time.

1917 Marcel
Duchamp (1887–
1968) "finds,"
signs, and exhibits
his *Fountain.*
It is a urinal.

1919 Walter
Gropius takes over
the school of arts and
crafts at Weimar and
famously renames it
the Bauhaus.

1920s~1930s
International Style
U.S. Modernism

The International Style: Architecture since 1922 *was
first published in 1932 in conjunction with an exhibition
at the Museum of Modern Art in New York. Written by
Philip JOHNSON (1906–) and the historian and critic
Henry-Russell Hitchcock, it included work by architects
such as Gropius, Le Corbusier, Rietveld, and Mies van
der Rohe and was instrumental in introducing the
new European architecture to the U.S.*

The German Pavilion for the 1929
International Exhibition in Barcelona,
designed by Mies van der Rohe.

The book sets out the esthetic
principles of the style using built
works to illustrate various points, and
it reads almost as a design guide. The
principles enumerated are "volume (space
enclosed by thin planes) rather than mass;
regularity as opposed to symmetry; elegant
materials; technical perfection, and fine
proportions in place of applied ornament."
The style is characterized by white flat
walls with no extra applied decoration,
severely cubic forms, large areas
of glazing, and open planning.

THE PEOPLE'S ARCHITECTURE
Henry-Russell Hitchcock had previously
used the term "International" in the U.S.,
to distinguish certain works from
"Modern" architecture or "the new
tradition," which, according to his
analysis, still showed evidence of a
continuity with the past—that is to say, a

1925 The Beaux-Arts-style Vanderbilt Mansion in New York, so recently a flagship for American Classicism à la Française, is demolished. It was so old-fashioned.

1927 In Paris, Adolf Loos builds a completely unornamented house using cube shapes for the arch-Dadaist Tristan Tzara.

1938–42 J.J.P. Oud abandons the severe tenets of De Stijl for a more playful style, in the Shell Building at The Hague. This style earns the nickname "Beton-Rococo."

concern with mass and ornament though perhaps with some simplification. The International Style had no continuity with the architectural past or with history, avoided decoration altogether, and placed emphasis on space and plane rather than mass.

The term had been used by Europeans in the context of the Socialist and Bolshevik Internationals who saw architecture as a fundamental part of the forming of a new social order. "International" represented an ideal of widening communities and an end of nationalism. The style had developed through different building types but was especially associated with research into new kinds of housing where the functional and social aspects of the design were of major importance. In the hands of the Americans it became a formula for an esthetic style not concerned with anything other than form. Twenty years later, however, Hitchcock wrote that the International Style had been "probably the

NAMES ON THE WALL

MoMA's Machine Art exhibition of 1934 was organized by **Philip Johnson** *to showcase modern mass-produced goods and new materials. Johnson's first architectural work to achieve critical acclaim was his New Canaan home (1949). Inspired by* **Mies van der Rohe***, it was a cube with glazed walls. Johnson did not constrain himself to a Modernist esthetic, and 30 years later his advocacy helped* **Michael Graves** *win the competition for a new city administration building in Portland, Oregon, a commission that signaled Postmodernism's absorption into America's architectural mainstream.*

major achievement of the 20th century." Its continued development in the U.S. has been mainly in the development of office buildings, where form is a part of corporate identity and buildings are representative of successful capitalism: ironic for a style that was originally motivated by social concerns.

The new school at Dessau (1926), designed by Gropius, was used to illustrate "a more extended articulation with more emphasis on the organic relation between the parts."

1925 Gramophone records bring the new jazz music into every home.

1926 Poetic, Modernist versions of the classics are pouring from the pen of Jean Cocteau.

1927 The horrible automobile death of avant-garde dancer Isadora Duncan shocks contemporary art lovers.

1925~1935
The Jazz Age
Art Deco

Art Deco was the popular version of the cool sophistication and austerity of early 1930s Modernism. Buildings have the same basically simple cubic forms relying on a juxtaposition of horizontal and vertical elements to create dramatic effect. The various volumes are usually articulated with "setback" stepped forms.

Many influences came to bear on the style that produced buildings such as Radio City Music Hall at Rockefeller Center, New York.

Instead of continuing the historicist/modernist debate, Art Deco accepted the new technologies, embraced the Bauhaus philosophy, and employed a rich variety of machine-inspired geometric decoration. Immensely popular, the style spread to fashion, furniture, and graphics and included influences from all areas of popular culture: streamlining inspired by the automobile, faceted and refracted images from the cinema, and the rhythms of jazz music.

The style, and its name, originated in Paris at the 1925 Exposition des Arts Décoratifs et Industriels Modernes. *Robert Mallet-Stevens* (1886–1945) was a founding member of the Union des Artistes Modernes who promoted the style in Europe.

In the U.S., where there was less reluctance to embrace new technologies, the "jazz" era saw the second wave of skyscrapers that were symbolic of the important new wealthy patrons: the big corporations. *Raymond Hood's* (1881–1934) McGraw-Hill Building in New York (1929) and the Empire State Building by Shreve, Lamb, and Harmon (1931) are examples of the new type. The most famous is the Chrysler Building (1929) by *William Van Alen* (1882–1954).

Sisters Are Doing It...

Some people call Art Deco effeminate because it was taken into the women's realm of fashion fabrics. Undeniably, the 1920s was the first age of female emancipation. In European art schools, many women became first-class citizens by virtue of the quality of their work. They were also good at putting on the style. Cropped hair, flat chests, slimline dresses: this androgynous look can be seen as a manifestation of Art Deco itself. Think of it as an all-around culture and see how high and low you can go.

1920s The word "flapper" is coined to describe the modern young women of the 1920s, with their bobbed hair and unconventional ways.

1929 The Museum of Modern Art opens in New York.

1933 Greta Garbo, the enigmatic Swedish actress, stars in *Queen Christina*.

With its homage to the automobile—its sparkling beaten metal doors, stainless steel panels, and gargoyles modeled on radiator caps—it has become the icon of Art Deco style.

Rockefeller Center introduced significant new urban design ideas. Set back from the streets, in the middle of the development, which covers three city blocks, the offices are grouped into the slenderest, soaring RCA building. The street level provides, for the first time, public open spaces

Rockefeller Center's central skyscraper, the RCA (now GE) Building (1934) is 70 storeys high. In the foreground is Paul Manship's statue of Prometheus.

ut of Egypt

ncient Egypt was a ajor inspiration for rt Deco, especially in e U.S. The idea is nderstandable if we st glance at the Nile alley: the pyramids, e columns at Luxor, e richly encrusted mbs of the Pharoahs, e painted colors f Egypt. When utankhamen's tomb as discovered in 923 a whole new epertoire came into ay. Buildings abound U.S. cities with this nd of decoration, ut it would be hard identify specific ources. There are ome truly Egyptian bjects, mostly ecorative, like the ythical beasts at decorate the ntrance lobbies nd upper limits of merican towers.

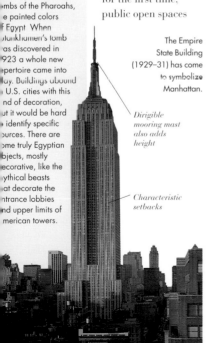

The Empire State Building (1929–31) has come to symbolize Manhattan.

Dirigible mooring mast also adds height

Characteristic setbacks

and a shopping mall. Inside, Radio City Music Hall is the epitome of 1930s opulence, its exotic timber veneers, bold patterns, reflective mirrors, and polished metalwork glittering in the skillfully subtle lighting.

NAMES ON THE WALL

The Hoover factory (Western Avenue, London) by **Wallis, Gilbert and Partners** *(1932–38) must stand here for all the glorious Art Deco factory frontages, many of which are now demolished, that sprang up along main roads in the south of England in the 1920s and 1930s. With its classically inclined façade, brilliant colors, and starburst entrance, it exudes confidence—a fitting place to make new goods for a new age.*

1956 Pop art emerges on the scene, with a blend of commercial images and intellectual take-off points.

1955 The world of youth is jumping and jiving to Bill Haley's "Rock Around the Clock."

1955 Concrete hits music. *Musique concrète*, with its recorded mix of musical and natural sounds, makes performances and performers redundant.

1950s
Et Tu Brute?
Brutalism

The expression "New Brutalism" originated in Britain in 1954 and was attributed to Alison and Peter SMITHSON (b. 1928 and 1923), who, like many other young architects in Europe, were frustrated by the problems of getting work in a profession dominated by the established older generation. The term referred, perhaps mockingly, to the puritanical approach of a younger generation committed to the extreme Modernist principles of the visible, honest expression of structures and materials.

New uses for old concrete mixers.

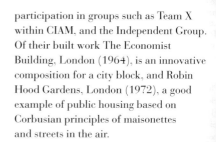

The Smithsons' High School at Hunstanton, in Norfolk, was inspired by the work for MIT by Mies van der Rohe.

Hunstanton School in Norfolk (1949–54) is the original British Brutalist building. Here the Smithsons took their ideas of truth to materials to the extreme. They exposed not only the materials of construction but also the services: the pipes, conduits, and fixings. They have had enormous influence both through their buildings and by participation in groups such as Team X within CIAM, and the Independent Group. Of their built work The Economist Building, London (1964), is an innovative composition for a city block, and Robin Hood Gardens, London (1972), a good example of public housing based on Corbusian principles of maisonettes and streets in the air.

1957 The Beat Generation is making its voice heard. Jack Kerouac's *On the Road* is published.

1959–63 The British architects Stirling and Gowan are at their most politely brutal in their design for the Department of Engineering at Leicester University.

1962 The first communications satellite, *Telstar*, is launched by the U.S., and has a song named after it by The Tornados.

EUROPEAN BRUTES

The other use of the term Brutalism is derived from the French *béton brut*, literally translated as unfinished or raw concrete. In contrast to the prim, cool cubic forms of 1930s Modernism that exploited the monolithic qualities of concrete to make precise, white, machinelike planes and surfaces, by the late 1940s and 1950s architects were beginning to experiment with the "plastic" properties of concrete. With adequate steel reinforcement, it could be poured on site into any shape and in variable thicknesses to form curves and slopes. Moreover, its surface could take on any number of textures, mirroring the surface of the "shutter," the formwork of wood or metal into which the concrete was poured.

Several of Le Corbusier's buildings fall into this category, reflecting his move away from the rationalist formalism of early Modernism. The Unité d'Habitation at Marseilles, the culmination of Le Corbusier's ambition to reinvent the idea of a town or suburb within one structure, was realized in concrete. The basic structure, including the enormous angled *pilotis* that hold it above ground, is formed of concrete cast in situ. The knots in the wood used to make the shutters are clearly visible, giving a surreal texture to the surface.

Brutalism

The term Brutalism encapsulates just a moment rather than a movement: a short-lived period when the frank expression of concrete monumentality was deemed both needful and desirable. The use of a brutalist aesthetic on London's South Bank seems ironic when it is remembered that the Festival of Britain, which had previously occupied the site, was intended to mark an emphatic end to wartime drabness. The uninviting walkways and gray spaces are now generally deemed to be unsuccessful, but never mind, Denys Lasdun's National Theatre really does look lovely lit up at night.

The exterior of the Hayward Gallery, London (1964), has a combination of precast and in-situ concrete surfaces.

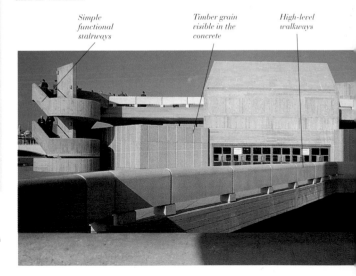

Simple functional stairways

Timber grain visible in the concrete

High-level walkways

1953 The theory of plate tectonics is developed. Six large plates and a number of small ones fit neatly together to form Earth's crust. Volcanoes and earthquakes occur along the "joints" of the plates.

1956 The neutrino (a particle with no electric charge and no, or very little, mass) is finally detected in solar radiation. Physicists had been trying to pin it down since its existence was surmised in 1931.

1958 French anthropologist Claude Lévi-Strauss (1908–90) writes *Structural Anthropology*, developing his theory of Structuralism, which suggests a universal structure common to all societies.

1950~1970

Serious Structuralists
Order à la Carte

According to the Structuralists, Modern movement architecture is too bland, ill-defined spatially, neutral, and difficult to inhabit. Expressionism or Formalism is the opposite—too subjective, emotive, and idiosyncratic. The Structuralists proposed something between the two: an intelligible complexity. A nonhierarchical "structural" framework provides the order within which there is some flexibility, allowing individual choice.

Dutch Treat
Hertzberger's Centraal Beheer in Apeldoorn has been identified as one of the seminal office buildings of the twentieth century, and his ability to humanize by fragmenting large interior spaces is equally evident in the Vredenburg Music Center. There have been comments on Hertzberger's slightly surprising but intentionally antielitist use of mundane industrial materials like concrete blocks, which have a tendency to attract graffiti. But, hey, the same critic asserts that Hertzberger's built forms are strongly defined and robust enough to take it!

Centraal Beheer offices, Apeldoorn, Netherlands (Herman Hertzberger), provides user-friendly spaces for staff both externally and internally.

The movement is largely limited to Holland and to architects such as *Aldo Van Eyck* (1918–), *Herman Hertzberger* (1932–), and *Piet Blom* (1934–), although the basic idea, to include individual variety and complexity within a structured or ordered framework, can be identified in the work of other modern architects. Between 1959 and 1963 Aldo Van Eyck, with Hertzberger and Joseph Bakema, edited the journal *Forum*, an important mouthpiece for the movement. Both Van Eyck and Bakema were members of Team X who had challenged the authority and relevance of CIAM in 1956, the end of its second period of great influence.

1966 *Mlle. Ravpoux,* a portrait by Dutch artist Vincent van Gogh (1853–90), sells for 150,000 guineas ($441,000.00) at Christie's in London.

1969 British chemist Dorothy Hodgkin (b.1910) works out the three-dimensional structure of the tiny insulin molecule.

1974 The U.S. moon program ends, and scientific resources are diverted to environmental research.

The Kunsthal in Rotterdam (1992)—a square crossed by inclined ramps—by the supercool Office for Metropolitan Architecture.

STRUCTURALIST STRUCTURES

The Apeldoorn offices of the Centraal Beheer by Hertzberger (1968–74), based on the idea of office as community, are modeled on a cell-like honeycomb structure. All the interior spaces are only partially enclosed, still visibly part of the whole— the excitement of labyrinthine space without the fear of being lost. The exterior is unusual for "offices"—a jumble of small cubes jostled together, more like the image of a Mexican Indian village. The Municipal Orphanage (1958–60) by Aldo Van Eyck was conceived as a small city with different-sized buildings. Piet Blom's "Kasbah" housing scheme in Hengelo (1965–73) and 't Speelhuis community center and housing in Helmond (1975–78) show a development of Structuralism in town planning, with densely clustered houses and free-flowing open spaces.

What Is It?

Structuralism, a movement in human sciences, originated with the linguist Ferdinand de Saussure (1857–1913), who said that language is a structure, "a system of signification" or "code," that holds meaning only in relation to itself. The anthropologist Claude Lévi-Strauss (1908–90) extended the idea to include all cultural processes. Ahistorical, basic structures underlie the architectural process in the same way; design is merely a process of searching for them.

1938 Mies van der Rohe becomes professor of architecture in Chicago and infuses students with Modernist ideas.

1948 In Britain the first National Health Service comes into being. It offers no cure for the shock of the new.

1950 Jackson Pollock is making his mark with his Abstract Expressionist drip paintings to hang on the clean new walls.

1930~2000
Glass Menageries
Skyscrapers

Tall buildings defy stylistic classification. As a type, they are usually glass-skinned and air-conditioned—familiar bland forms in cities all over the world, frequently only noticeable as they assume, if but briefly, the title of "tallest building in the world." Since the early tall buildings of the Chicago School and the 1930s in the U.S., few have provoked the same excitement as the Empire State Building or achieved the same tectonic quality as Mies's Seagram Building.

Lever House in New York (1952), which organizes the offices into a glass-skinned slab set back from the street and raised above a two-story podium, has been imitated by many. Its architects, *Louis SKIDMORE* (1897–1962), *Nathaniel OWINGS* (1903–84), and *John MERRILL* (1896–1975), who were uniquely organized on a commercial model known as SOM, established their reputation with this building. Since the firm's development of sophisticated steel-framing techniques, SOM has completed many more, including the John Hancock Center in Chicago (1970), which was the first to include different uses in one tower, and the Sears Tower (1974), at 1,500 feet tall.

The World Trade Center in New York (1974) by *Minoru YAMASAKI* (1912–) has two identical towers, square in plan and beautifully proportioned. The façades,

Building tapers as it rises

After 25 years of building skyscrapers the Chicago firm Skidmore, Owings, and Merrill were still innovating, as at the John Hancock Center, Chicago, 1970.

External, cross-braced frame

The rigid frame has no internal supports

1952 To coincide with the explosion of office buildings in American cities, the U.S. tests the first H bomb. The mushroom-cloud generation wonders what to make of it.

1956 While architecture is clean and crisp, John Osborne's *Look Back in Anger* characters are still sitting around in old-fashioned kitchens.

1957 After Jack Kerouac's *On the Road* is published, the word "beatnik" enters the language and the Beat movement spreads to Paris.

unusually, are structural with wide, closely spaced mullions, which give an appearance of solidity and dramatically reflect the sun. Their precarious siting on the very edge of Manhattan Island has unfortunately been obscured by the collection of mediocre Postmodern buildings that now fills the reclaimed land at their base. (The stone removed for the very deep foundations was used to build extra land around the island.)

NEW DEVELOPMENTS

The skyscraper is still fertile territory for technological research. In a proposal for a tall building in Shanghai, China, Kenneth Yeang has suggested reductions in energy consumption. With the skyscraper's sealed skin, an air-conditioned interior would seem inevitable. However, a double-layered façade allows different parts to be opened during different seasons for ventilation and heat control. "Sky courts," several stories high and planted with trees, oxygenate the air. The design for this complex multilayered façade is not just a response to functional requirements or climatic controls, but is also an attempt to evoke memories of Chinese tradition.

Yamasaki's World Trade Center, New York, with its smooth twin towers, perhaps marks the summit of his work.

The Tallest? Not Quite.

It had to come. The tallest buildings in the world seem to have been designed by one man, Cesar Pelli (b.1926), whose twin skyscrapers in Kuala Lumpur are now counted higher than his unlovely, vertical, 800-foot stainless-steel-clad obelisk at London's Canary Wharf, the tallest in Britain, and the second tallest in Europe. The title of "tallest building in the world" changes periodically, and because of the skyscraper mentality the title seems to have mostly stayed in the U.S. At 985 feet the Eiffel Tower is puny compared with the Empire State Building: not the first to head heavenward at 1,250 feet. As for Yamasaki's World Trade Center towers (1,350 feet), they have long been surpassed. And of course there are other contenders—the tallest business center, bank, residential building, and so on. From ground level they all look fabulous; from nine floors up in Manhattan some of them look plain stupendous. It's part of a mystique that stretches from Asia to California.

Going Underground

From the perspective of the late twentieth century we should also mention the development of Earth scrapers. By the mid-1980s, 5,000 American families were living at least partially underground, and there were 27 subterranean schools in Oklahoma. Excavating makes good sense where weather conditions are severe, land is precious, or planning controls are extreme. The British architect Arthur Quarmby inhabits an earth-sheltered building in Yorkshire (completed 1975). There hasn't exactly been a rush to follow, but as the environment deteriorates, more of us will be joining the tunneling ecoactivists.

1966 Floods ravage
northern Italy; priceless art
treasures destroyed in
Florence and Venice.

1967 Robert Venturi
publishes *Complexity and
Contradiction* ... and the
first discovery is made of
pulsating stars, or pulsars.

1968 Troubled times:
the assassination of the
civil rights crusader
Martin Luther King,
while campaigning for
racial equality in the
deep South.

1966
Be Reasonable
Neorationalists

*The intellectual principles of Neorationalism are
a combination of Renaissance theories and early
twentieth-century ideas of reason and logic. Beauty
is a result of order, truth, and reason, not Baroque
illusion or Expressionist symbolism. Architecture,
as a science, has its own natural laws, which can
be recovered from analysis of the sprawling city
as the physical embodiment of history, and
buildings as a series of archetypes.*

This contemporary movement is
associated primarily with Italian and
German architects. *Aldo Rossi* (1931–) is
the principal advocate. He published his
theory *L'architettura della città* in 1966,
followed by *Architettura razionale* (with
other contributors) in 1973. Opposed to
the "false embalming process" of historical
restoration, his buildings are carefully
considered in the context of the
surrounding structures of the city
to create a new circumstance.

O. M. Ungers's drawing
for the Frankfurt Trade
Fair Hall gateway.

THEATER OF LIFE

The residential development in the
Gallaretese Quarter in Milan (1969–78) is
a bold composition with a façade that is
almost completely open, with arcades at
street level and loggias and courts above,
allowing direct physical contact between
residents and shoppers in the adjacent

NAMES ON THE WALL

Rossi's Architecture of the City *and* **Jane
Jacobs's** Death and Life of Great American
Cities *(1961) emphasized the lived
experience of urban spaces and the
importance of diversity in the city's fabric.
They gave weight to arguments for
rehabilitation rather than redevelopment
of declining building stock.* **J. P. Kleihues**
*fought for the Altbau (rehabilitation)
section of the 1977 IBA project in Berlin,
which better respected the economic needs
and esthetic wishes of Berliners. What
does it say about architecture and ego
that the Altbau projects went strangely
unreported in the architectural press?*

1969 DDT was not the answer to agriculture's prayers. In the U.S. the toxic substance is banned.

1971–76 Aldo Rossi designs his masterwork, a cemetery at Modena; building will not begin until 1980.

1973 East and West Germany establish diplomatic relations for the first time since partition.

Excuse Me, Dr. Gropius...Can We Have a Few Words?

Neorationalism really dishes Gropius. His Bauhaus ideology rejected historical architecture, and replaced it with a total emphasis on the individual's imagination. Not that imagination's bad, but your brain goes funny if you do too much. Three influential books published between 1961 and 1969 independently challenged Onkel Walter. Two Americans—Jane Jacobs and Robert Venturi—and an Egyptian, Hassan Fathy, criticized the architecture of glass, steel, and concrete from their own vantage points (New York, Princeton, and Cairo). They broadly disavowed impersonal high-rises, and advocated forms of architecture that were truly vernacular, in which people (remember them?) and the function and purpose of specific buildings were actually taken into consideration. Odd, that.

street market. In his primary school building in Falgano Olana (1972) there are other clues to what Rossi calls "the theater of life" that have a reading in two directions. The courtyard steps are also the seats for the school photographs; a huge clock tells the present time but also refers to the time of childhood; the books that contain knowledge are contained within the cylindrical form of the library, which is contained within the internal courtyard of the school, the playground for the children. The theatrical idea —the reciprocity between the audience that watches and that at the same time is watched—appears

Aldo Rossi's drawing of the Teatro del Mondo, Venice (1979), which floated temporarily on the lagoon.

constantly in his works, including his many drawings.

In Germany the Neorationalist movement is represented by *O. M. Ungers* (1926–), *J. P. Kleihues* (1933–), and the *Krier* brothers, *Leon* (1946–) and *Robert* (1938–). Under the directorship of Kleihues, the Berlin IBA offered an opportunity to implement urban ideas on a large scale. The exhibition uses a catalog of rational typologies or archetypes to describe the different projects, such as "corner house," "row house," "gateway buildings," or "urban villa." On Friedrichstrasse an "open block plan" has eight "urban villas," based on an eighteenth-century model. The "villas," designed by Rossi, Grassi, and Hollein, are actually small apartment buildings and are all the same basic size and shape. Green spaces and buildings are all treated as separate parts that make up the whole.

1920 Promodernist students at Tokyo Imperial University rebel and form the Japanese Secession.

1923 An earthquake in Kanto leaves Frank Lloyd Wright's Imperial Hotel standing and proves the strength of steel and concrete.

1952-55 The birth control pill is discovered; it is soon to change the lives of women in the Western world.

1950s
Big in Japan
Japanese Architecture

Modern Japanese culture has had a great influence on contemporary Western architecture. Frank Lloyd Wright built the Juyokaken Kindergarten (1921) and the Imperial Hotel in Tokyo (1922), and Bruno Taut wrote about Japanese culture and architecture. The history of the growth of Modernism in Japan is similar to that in Europe and North America. The earliest modern buildings started to appear, as an alternative to traditional building, in the 1920s. By the 1930s a call for a Japanese national style had resulted in a hybrid—bare classical forms with curved roofs imitating traditional timber construction.

Tokyo's Nagakin Capsule Tower, built in 1972, shows Kurokawa's Metabolist theories in action.

Hi-tech adaptability

Sci-fi pods project from the core

The capsule is the key

Kenzo TANGE (1913–) was vociferous in his criticism of both nostalgic historicism and boring international Modernism, stating "only the beautiful can be functional." His work uses symbolic form based on Japanese tradition, combined with modern technology. He was recognized as an important figure in the Modern movement when he was invited to present his winning entry for the Hiroshima Peace Center (1949–56) at the 1951 CIAM. Later projects continued to develop urban core systems and the idea of components.

Too Many People

During the late 1960s, light began to dawn in some areas that certain places on this damaged little orb were facing serious overpopulation, especially in some American, and several Japanese, cities. The problem still remains. However, the American moon landing of July 1968 caught some people's imagination sufficiently powerfully to allow them to fantasize about the colonization of the solar system. Yes, it's an old chestnut (remember those 1950s bubble-gum cards?), but with the recent (1998) announcement concerning water on the moon, you can bet the space architects are sharpening their pencils ... they may even be drawing as you read this.

1958–61 Kunio Maekawa, former collaborator of Le Corbusier, builds the Municipal Assembly Hall in Tokyo in the platform-on-stilts style.

1959 Alain Resnais's film *Hiroshima Mon Amour* (made in France and Japan) tells of a French actress falling in love with a Japanese architect.

1966 Already a well-known designer, Mary Quant brings her most famous creation, the miniskirt, to the world of fashion.

METABOLISM

Under Tange's direction, the Metabolist group had great influence on architectural production and theory during the 1960s and early 1970s, primarily in establishing the importance, especially in urban situations, of the relationship between the public realm and private spaces. The Nagakin Capsule Tower in Tokyo (1972), by *Noria KUROKAWA* (1934–), shows a culmination of these ideas and is typical of the futuristic and science-fictionlike imagery of his work. The tower stands as part of the infrastructure of the city. Living units are mass-produced, minimal "pods," or "capsules," clustered around it.

Kidosaki House, Tokyo, by Tadeo Ando. This architect helped to revolutionize the Japanese house.

AN OUTDOOR LIVING ROOM

In a series of wonderful houses and chapels built during the 1980s, *Tadeo ANDO* (1941–) established himself as an accomplished architect, rejecting Metabolism and returning to Le Corbusier, *Louis KAHN* (1901–74), and early Modernism for inspiration. Spaces and forms have a simple purity, evolved in relation to the landscape. The poured concrete he uses is beautifully detailed.

NAMES ON THE WALL

Charlotte Perriand *accepted an invitation to spend time in Japan advising on design policy in relation to export goods in 1940. One of the seemingly unlikely outcomes of this venture was a version of the iconic Modernist tubular steel chaise-longue built using bamboo! During the 1970s, Japanese architecture was dominated by architects such as* **Arata Isozaki** *(1931–) and* **Kazuo Shinohara** *(1925–), both with a more Postmodern approach of Neomannerist abstract compositions, semicircular and cubic forms, typified by gigantic scale.*

Indigestible: Metabolism

There's a bizarre poetry in the idea that the nation that gave us everything from the bullet train to the direness of the manga comic could also give us an architecture so futuristic that it eventually fuded into the wallpaper. At the root of Japanese Metabolism was the concept that, like skin, architecture could change and be replaced. That's why the tower-and-pod idea was so important for its success. The austere "pods" were usually clustered around a central building.

1972 The American president, Richard Nixon, visits China and Russia. In this year, he is re-elected in a landslide victory.

1973 Chinese-American actor Bruce Lee starts a martial arts craze with his kung fu films, such as *Enter the Dragon*.

1974 *The Godfather Part II*, directed by Francis Ford Coppola, wins the Academy Award for Best Picture .

1972~1990
Very Cool
Postmodernism

Cool, regular, symmetrical façade

Classical (-ish dream topping

The specific task of the architect, according to Charles Jencks in his Language of Postmodern Architecture *(1977), is "seeing that the environment is sensual, humorous, surprising, and coded as a readable text." The way to achieve this was to abandon the universal notions of Modernism derived from functionalism and rationalism. Postmodernism embraces an architecture that is clearly derived from the familiar, the historical, and the vernacular. The result is an ambiguous, and often ironic, "radical eclecticism." The recipe: take easily recognizable bits of buildings (which are often Classical) from a whole variety of places and eras, and reuse them at will.*

Overall symmetry and uniformity of elements is mixed with a jovial reference to Classical devices in Philip Johnson and John Burgee's AT & T Building, New York.

P*hilip JOHNSON* (1906–), who began by promoting the International Style in the 1930s, became one of the leaders of Postmodernism 40 years later. His AT&T Building in New York (1978–83, with John Burgee) is most often used to illustrate the style: a modern skyscraper with a principal façade of Classical symmetry and composition. The arched, semicircular central entrance is flanked by smaller openings. The framed structure is disguised

Robert Venturi

Robert Venturi (1925–) provided the theoretical basis for Postmodernism with his books *Complexity and Contradiction in Architecture* (1966) and *Learning from Las Vegas* with Denise Scott-Brown and Steven Izenour, published in 1972. Against the purity and simplicity of International Style, he argued for "complexity" and "ambiguity." To Mies's statement "less is more," he replied, "less is a bore." From small projects, his built work has recently grown to include prestigious projects such as the extension to the National Gallery in London's Trafalgar Square (1986).

by masonry in imitation of Classical stonework. At the top an attic story is crowned with a jokey oversized pediment with an open top.

FUN, FUN, FUN

Criticism of Modernism for its blandness, anonymity, and bogus functionalism had increased both in the U.S. and in Europe, especially following problems with social housing schemes. Postmodernism, with its legible, familiar forms, was expected to provide a workable alternative. *Ricardo Bofill's* (1939–) housing schemes in France, such as Les Arcades du Lac St. Quentin-en-Yvelines (1972–75) and Les Espaces d'Abraxas Marne-La-Vallée (1978–83), employ monumental forms, which Bofill believes promote a sense of intimacy and collective identity. The façades are composed of simplified concrete versions of Classical carved motifs, with bizarre alterations.

Bofill's earlier work, with the *Taller de Arquitectura* group in Spain, was much more interesting. A large-scale housing project in Barcelona, Walden Seven (1970–75), uses industrial forms and a more romantic imagery —half-built or half-ruined. With no rules, no expanded theory, and a reliance on commercialism and taste, Postmodernism has been condemned as mere kitsch by European architects favoring other developments within Modernism.

Les Espaces d'Abraxas (1978–83), Bofill's attempt to transform the Classical orders to a contemporary language.

1969 The American Neil Armstrong becomes the first man on the moon. This leads indirectly to aluminum foil and Teflon appearing in all our kitchens.

1974 The extraordinary Pompidou Centre goes up in Paris, and is a great conversation piece.

1980s International film festivals foster art movies. Foster and Rogers are able to watch Kurosawa's action-packed *Seven Samurai*.

1980s
Hi-Tech
Rogers and Foster

Buildings that look like machinery, with hard, shiny, metallic surfaces, industrial elements like gantries and walkways, and moving parts, are described as Hi-Tech. Structures are often exposed. Overall forms and

Crescent wing of the Sainsbury Centre for the Visual Arts, Norwich, by Norman Foster.

shapes of different elements are not notably different from those seen in other modern buildings, but the palette of materials includes those associated with other technologies like industrial production or aerospace research. Hi-Tech's reliance on only the visual means is often considered a self-conscious stylization.

Future systems
The family house designed in 1993/4 by Future Systems (Jan Kaplicky and Amanda Levete) can only be described as out of the ordinary. Apart from solid walls, the rest is in glass, the north side, facing the street, in translucent blocks, the south, garden side, inclined and transparent to let in the sun. The materials and finishes are crisp and sharp, with aluminum stairs and white ceramic floor tiles adding to the ephemeral qualities of lightness and fragility.

The model of Hi-Tech is the CNAC (Centre National d'Art et Culture, formerly the Centre Pompidou) in Paris (1974), designed by *Renzo Piano* (1937–) and *Sir Richard Rogers* (1933–). Escalators in curved glass tubes climb the five stories, precariously cantilevered on the outside of the glass façade between the huge steel girders of the structure. Inside, the ground floor is all hustle and bustle, with bookshops and ticket sales and temporary exhibitions forming an extension of the piazza outside; beyond, there is emptiness. Flexibility—the ability to change internal layouts of rooms—was an important concern during the 1970s.

Putting all the structures and services on the outside of a building achieved this: the internal space can be adapted to suit any kind of temporary exhibition. Rogers developed this model, in which the display of services and structure is of fundamental importance, with such buildings as Lloyds Bank Building (1979–84) and the Channel 4 offices (1990), both in London.

1980 John Lennon, former member of The Beatles, is shot dead by a psychopath outside his home in New York.

1980 The "extinct" coelacanth is found alive and well, 600 feet / 180 meters below the sea surface.

1980s Yuppies (Young Urban Professionals) become the symbol of a money-making decade.

Get on the right track, baby

In 1960 six young architects, Peter Cook (1936–), Ron Herron (1930–), Michael Webb (1937–), David Greene (1937–), Warren Chalk (1927–), and Dennis Crompton (1935–) formed Archigram—literally, "architecture in drawing." They are advocates of the new technology's expendability in building and interior design. The first exhibition of their work "Living City" was in 1963 at London's Institute of Contemporary Arts. Archigram revolutionized British architectural thinking before the group dispersed in 1970.

Another important early Hi-Tech building is the Sainsbury Centre for the Visual Arts in Norwich (1977) by Rogers's contemporary and one-time colleague, *Sir Norman FOSTER* (1935–). In a less flamboyant vein, there is the Financial Times Print Works, London (1988), by *Nicholas GRIMSHAW* (1939–), where the moving print machinery is visible through the glazed façade.

The Lloyds Building in London (1979–84) by Richard Rogers.

NAMES ON THE WALL

The work of British husband-and-wife team **Alison** *and* **Peter Smithson** *should be mentioned in this context. They showed their design for a "House of the Future" at the* Daily Mail *Ideal Home Exhibition in London in 1956. The exhibit predicted a future with mass-produced accommodation units and sophisticated household technology including remote control, microwave ovens, and, best of all, a portable electrostatic dust collector that would operate independently of human intervention throughout the house.*

ORIGINS

The origins of Hi-Tech can be linked to the work of the American *Richard BUCKMINSTER FULLER*, (1895–1983), and to the group of English architects called Archigram. Buckminster Fuller built little, but his ideas had enormous influence through his teaching. Projects for a Dymaxion (dynamic and maximum efficiency) House (1927) and for a Dymaxion Three-wheeled Auto (1933), were a real attempt to cast off the history and esthetics of convention to deal with production only in the modern context. He went on to develop geodesic domes, which were similarly ahistorical, using a standardized kit of parts. The best-known dome is the U.S. Pavilion built for Expo '67, held in Montreal.

1968 British government abandons £55 million plan for London's third airport at Stansted in Essex; but plans will be back on Sir Norman Foster's drawing board before the end of the millennium.

1969 Ludwig Mies van der Rohe, doyen of the Bauhaus, dies.

1969 An avant-garde art movement, Land Art, is committed to making art out of elements of nature, such as earth and rocks.

1968-1995

Postmodern Formalism
The New York Five

The work of the Neo-Corbusian New York Five was first exhibited at the Museum of Modern Art in New York in 1969. Their early works, the "white" houses, imitate the form of International Style buildings, with simple volumes and white, flat surfaces. The concrete was replaced with the "traditional" timber frames and boarding of American houses.

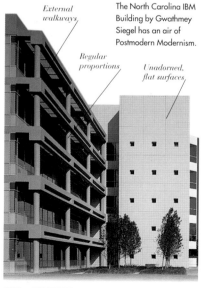

External walkways

The North Carolina IBM Building by Gwathmey Siegel has an air of Postmodern Modernism.

Regular proportions

Unadorned, flat surfaces

Drawing on Italian Rationalism, *Peter Eisenman's* (1932–) early work is preoccupied with meaning in form. His contempt for the idea that architecture should be merely "functional" is clear in his series of houses, which he numbers as if they are art works. Number VI, the Frank House (1972), has a staircase that cannot be climbed, that leads nowhere. *Michael Graves's* (1934–) concern with form has developed away from the Rationalist view toward the more obvious Postmodern neohistoricism, as seen in the Public Services Building in Portland, Oregon.

Charles Gwathmey (1938–), in practice since 1971 with *Robert Siegel*, has designed numerous private houses, including his own at Amagansett in New York's Long Island (1965–67), as well as public buildings such as the East Campus of Columbia University in New York City (1981).

1973 In Vietnam, the U.S. government hoists the white flag and a cease-fire is agreed upon on January 28; the last American troops leave on March 29. America loses its first war abroad.

1977 The film *Saturday Night Fever* hits the screen. John Travolta becomes an overnight icon in a white suit.

1980 The New York Five (aka "the Whites") disband.

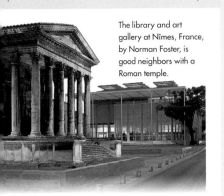

The library and art gallery at Nîmes, France, by Norman Foster, is good neighbors with a Roman temple.

SITE

The multidisciplinary group SITE (Sculpture In The Environment) was set up by the sculptor James Wines (1932–), with the intention to move away from "functionalism" toward a unity with art. It is best known for a series of supermarkets for the BEST chain in the U.S., all of which deliberately disrupt in a jokey way. The Peeling Project in Richmond, Virginia (1971–72), has brickwork peeling away from the elevation. The Tilt Showroom in Towson (1976–78) has the whole façade lifted at a rakish angle above the ground.

The most prolific of the five is *Richard MEIER* (1934–). As well as numerous individual houses and housing projects, he has completed public buildings such as the Museum of Applied Art in Frankfurt-am-Main (1979–80) and the Getty Museum in Los Angeles (1984). The most interesting of the five is *John HEJDUK* (1929–). He has a far more experimental approach, as shown by his alterations to the Cooper Union School in New York (1975) and his IBA housing in Berlin.

Richard Meier's Douglas House at Harbor Springs, Michigan.

visibly uses the same form as the structure opposite, the Maison Carrée, one of Europe's best preserved Roman temples. Meanwhile, his design for London's third airport, at Stansted (1992), is a simple rectangle in plan and puts all the workings of the building at low level. Free from the paraphernalia of ductwork and pipes, the simple roof, supported on a grid of branching tree-like columns, allows the concourse to be filled with natural daylight. Glazed walls afford views to the airfield and aircraft taking off and landing.

EUROPE

Early Norman Foster buildings are always classified with the Hi-Tech style of Sir Richard Rogers. However, Foster's more recent work is harder to classify. The library and art gallery at Nîmes in France (1993)

1960 Psychiatry has its mavericks too. R. D. Laing publishes *The Divided Self* and soon has a big following.

1970s Jamaican reggae music becomes popular in Britain. One of its leading exponents is Bob Marley.

1989 Leon Krier is chosen to plan the Prince of Wales's rather sinister model village, Poundbury, in Dorchester, Dorset.

1990s

How Does It Feel?
Sensual Response and Sustainability

The canopied stand at Lords Cricket Ground in London by Sir Michael and Patti Hopkins.

The way we perceive a place is not just a visual experience. The form of the building is important but the textures, smells, and sounds play an equal or greater role. The combination of these sensory experiences—the way wood feels to the touch and the resonance of our footsteps as we walk across the polished timber floor—are a major part of our reading of a place. This concern for the sensual quality of the materials (a phenomenological

appraisal rather than a stylistic classification), together with recent concerns for sustainability and disdain for increasing globalization, has inspired different architectures in response to specific locations and climates, and gives us another way to look at buildings.

The recent work of *Sir Michael HOPKINS* (1935–), who was associated with Hi-Tech in the 1970s and early 80s, is now very different. The Mound Stand at Lords Cricket Ground in London (1987), firmly rooted in the ground with load-bearing brick colonnades, physically and metaphorically rises up through enclosed levels to open up again beneath light white fabric canopies, like so many umbrellas that come out on a wet day at the game. More recently, the Glyndebourne Opera House (1994) uses bricks (the local material) and mortar with traditional

laying technique which make continuity possible without the expansion joints of modern brickwork. In the interior, curved and polished plywood, the material of so many musical instruments, is used for seats and balustrades.

FUKSAS

In France the work of the Italian architect *Massimiliano FUKSAS* shows the same consideration for location and for materiality. In the densely populated Bastille area of Paris, the Rue de Candie Sports Center (1994) fills a ragged site

1989 The deconstruction of the Berlin Wall is a cause for much rejoicing.

1990 The Hubble space telescope detects a huge storm system on Saturn. Astronomers name it the Great White Spot.

1990s New Age beliefs and alternative health practices become popular.

NAMES ON THE WALL

In the postwar period, Italy made a name for the successful refurbishment of museum spaces, requiring acute sensitivity to materials and sensory awareness.
Carlo Scarpa*'s work on the medieval Castelvecchio in Verona exemplifies this success. His skillful deployment of space, deft manipulation of light, and thoughtful placement of objects have created a place in which past and present coexist graciously, providing the visitor with occasional drama and the delight of beautifully executed details.*

roofs. The Maison des Arts at Michel de Montaigne University in Bordeaux (1997), also by Fuksas, again uses metal; this time the green color of oxidized copper covers the whole façade. Shutters contained within the skin modulate the surface, which is interrupted by two vertical slots of glass and a window running in a deep cut all the way around it.

with a series of interlinked volumes. The main structures are of raw concrete, with the sports hall wall exposed with a series of blind windows—recalling a familiar view of empty buildings in a city. The façade is clad with zinc panels that follow gentle curves, reminiscent of so many Mansard

Back To the Drawing Board

With the end of the millennium in sight, architects and planners remain incapable of agreement on concepts like "quality of life" and "the ecostructure," though all pay these issues lip service. The first has vainly eluded capture through time, while the second is in danger of becoming extinct. So, while the architects are busily trying to soothe the senses in larger building schemes, they must also now accommodate pressure from other directions, by incorporating degradables into construction. Come back, Metabolism! Consider, please: just what is a "caring" building? Can architecture ever be truly "green?" What restraints are we willing to impose on ourselves so that we can get "the balance" right? And whose balance are we talking about? The rocket is counting down. Now, how shall we wreck the Moon?

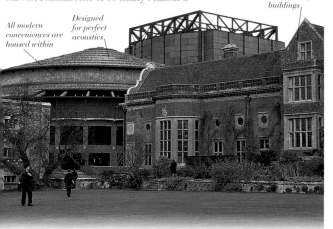

Harmonizes with existing buildings

All modern conveniences are housed within

Designed for perfect acoustics

The new opera house at Glyndebourne, Sussex, is at home in its peaceful setting.

1898 America comes to blows with Spain over Cuba, and destroys the Spanish fleet at Manila.

1936 The Spanish Civil War begins. Franco is appointed Chief of State. He takes control of the government in 1939.

1939 Franco's government is recognized by Britain, France, and the USA. The Spanish Civil War comes to an end.

1970~1990

Viva España
Spanish Regionalism

"Critical regionalism" is Kenneth Frampton's description of the development of Modernism in response to different physical and cultural contexts. Spain, following redemocratization, the introduction of legal protection for historic buildings, the staging of Expo in Seville in 1992 and the Olympic Games in Barcelona, has had the opportunity to reassert a cultural presence in Europe with major new buildings.

The arches of the airport buildings in Sev by José Rafael Moneo are characteristic Moorish features.

The architecture at the Seville Expo was very different from the previous one in Osaka in 1970, with its Metabolists, Archigram, and pneumatic structures. In many exhibits, a concern for history and cultural identity was expressed through a specific materiality and formal metaphor. As well as the Expo site, Seville has a new airport by *José Rafael MONEO* (1939–) and a new railroad station by *Antonio CRUZ* and *Antonio ORTIZ*. Both buildings have solid masonry forms with arched structures, reminiscent of Moorish buildings, in pale terracotta colors.

Buildings in the old industrial areas of Barcelona have been inventively restored. Lapena and Torres Workshops and Josep Lluis Mateos sports hall both occupy redundant factories.

GLORIOUS GAUDÍ

Most of the work of Spain's best-known architect *Antoni GAUDÍ* (1852–1926) is in Barcelona. "The straight line belongs to men, the curved one to God"—his own assertion—is probably the best explanation of his work. In pursuit of his vision, his buildings demonstrate a unique and original use of materials and forms, a rejection of rigid geometry to determine form, and an inspired decorative ability.

The complexity and individuality of his work, with no precedent and no imitators, has meant a problem for historians looking for links between the past and the future. In the context of Art Nouveau, he is rated as a genius, the only one employing a three-dimensional version of a style often criticized for its superficiality. Relying

1960s Cheap flights to Europe make foreign sun accessible to many people; Spain becomes the number one destination.

1976 Spain gives up control of a former colonial area—the Sahara—and the territory is divided between Morocco and Mauritania.

1992 The Olympic Games are held in Spain. Athletes have to contend with high temperatures.

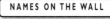

our Peaks

audí's Sagrada amilia church (begun 384) is his asterpiece, featuring ur 350-foot towers at are as much a presentation of gional Art Nouveau s they are an outright onder of the chitectural world. The alls and roof are of a in brickwork onstruction and the ain nave space has clined columns. If audí hadn't been hit y a tram, he might ve taught the ostmodernists a thing two about invention, e use of the past, and materials.

heavily on hand labor and craftwork, his work is also linked to the Arts and Crafts Movement in England and the Romantic *Modernisme* in Spain. Naturalistic or organic inspiration is evident but there are also similarities, in the depth and layering of the surfaces, with the rich geometric carvings of the Moorish palaces in southern Spain.

The façade of the Nativity (1893–1903), Church of the Sagrada Familia, Barcelona, by Gaudí. He began work on the church in 1884, and the building is still unfinished.

— *Elongated, openwork spires*

— *Riotous ornamentation*

NAMES ON THE WALL

*Other examples of locational sensitivity include **Álvaro Siza's** Center for Contemporary Galician Art in Santiago de Compostela (1993), **Antoine Predock's** Nelson Fine Arts Center at Arizona State University (1989), and **Ricardo Legorreta's** Museum of Contemporary Art in Monterey (1992). Siza uses granite, bright white marble, and stucco interiors to relate the site to the local built environment, Predock draws inspiration from local Spanish and Indian traditons, while Legorreta scales up a traditional courtyard house. Predock even managed to build with integrity in his Las Vegas Library and Discovery Museum (1990)!*

Something Old, Something New

Spain's a great symbol of the wonder and caprice of architecture. Given the remains of Moorish influence, the country's architecture has changed in response to economics. Conserve the medieval for locals and tourists alike, but flaunt the modern, with cheap concrete hotels

The appeal of the Moorish inheritance.

scarring miles of coastline. Nevertheless, the early 1990s chalked up notable successes in Spanish architecture, especially in Seville and in Barcelona, in time for the '92 Olympic Games. The Olympic Stadium itself (Gregotti with Correa & Mila) surreally transformed a pre-existing 1929 structure; the Olympic villages were horrible, but new town planning detail was better. Now, with the bubble burst, the Spanish are preserving and remodeling their older buildings. Hardly new, but fresh ideas can be usefully based on earlier statements.

1912 The term Minimalist comes into use in politics first. The Russian revolutionary Minimalists favor immediate post-revolutionary democracy.

1954 Anthony Caro begins to teach at St. Martin's School of Art in London; the cult of the impersonal grips a generation of sculptors.

1964 Modern art is in flight from interpretation, and the critic Susan Sontag's writing is the topic of conversation at intellectual dinner parties.

1960~1997

The Essence of Things
Minimalism

Freedom from clutter, from the distraction of trivia, allows concentration on the fundamental—the important qualities of form, of space, and of material. Here, beauty is not found in unnecessary adornment and distracting embellishment, but in the refinement of the essential heart of a building, the truly minimal. Simplicity and emptiness characterize such Minimalist architecture, recalling a monastic restraint.

The work of designers, according to the Minimalist architect *John PAWSON*, is to "clear up the chaotic world." This has been a concern since the late nineteenth century, but has become more pressing as a response to the "avalanche of consumerism." The photographs in Pawson's book *Minimum* (1996) provide an eloquent argument. Among the images are monasteries and convents, including Le Corbusier's Dominican friary of Sainte Marie-de-la-Tourette (1957–60) and the Cistercian Romanesque abbey at Le Thoronet. Pawson's Neuendorf house in Majorca (1989) uses the simple geometry of a cube, and the ocher coloring unites the building with its setting.

The Neuendorf house (1989) in Majorca by Silvestrin & Pawson is a perfect complement to its hot, dry setting. An air of intellectual repose is created by its confident forms.

PURE AND SIMPLE

Edouardo SOUTA DE MOURA (1952–) spent five years working for *Álvaro SIZA* (1933–), Portugal's best-known modern architect, whose work combines a Rationalist approach with a Mediterranean starkness. Souta De Moura works with simple forms and elegant detailing combined with the

Color enhances texture

Unadorned surfaces

1969 At an ICA exhibition subtitled Live in Your Head, Michael Craig-Martin's *4 Identical Boxes with Lids Reversed*, is not misdescribed.

1970s Minimalism is big in art with pared-down, nonreferential paintings and sculpture.

1980s Minimalist theories of interior design have a minimal impact as sales of Austrian blinds soar.

Honest to Goodness: Shaker Furniture

The Shakers are a religious sect, founded in England in the mid-1700s. Strongest in the U.S., especially during the 1840s, the Shakers became and remain famous for the functional simplicity of their furniture, usually of seasoned wood, smooth, with minimal fittings, sturdy but calm and capacious. The ideals behind their craftsmanship? Beauty rests in utility and every force evolves a form. And for those clinging to the Postmodern canon, hear this: "We have a right to improve the inventions of man, but not to vainglory or anything superfluous." Right on, Brothers and Sisters.

earthy richness of natural materials closely related to the traditional buildings of Portugal. The market building in Braga (1980–84) and the Cultural Center in Oporto (1981–88) both employ empty spatial simplicity and subtle natural materials. Typical of Souta De Moura's houses, the Bom Jesus House in Braga (1989–94) simply juxtaposes "a stone cube … and a concrete cube."
The Swiss architects

Jacques HERZOG (1950–) and *Pierre* DE MEURON (1950–) have developed their purist approach during the last twenty years, through a whole variety of different projects. The private collector's gallery in Munich (1991–92) (with Mario Meier) is a simple, freestanding, two-story rectangular block. Ingeniously dug into the ground, all that is visible of the "ground" floor are the clerestory windows all around. Clerestory windows on the upper level leave the solid band of plywood cladding suspended. The glass varies from opaque to reflective and back, depending on the light and the seasons. In 1996 they won the competition for the extension to London's Tate Gallery of Modern Art in the Bankside Power Station (1955) designed by Sir Giles Gilbert-Scott.

Simple, geometric shapes

NAMES ON THE WALL

Arguably the first European architect to articulate an esthetic of minimalism was the Austrian **Adolf Loos** *(1870–1933). He wrote numerous articles and essays, including* **Ornament and Crime** *in 1908. In this he lambasted historicism and labeled the urge to decorate "a pathology." He built several houses, including one in Paris for the Dadaist Tristan Tzara (1926), where he used beautifully simple forms, cleverly manipulated spaces, a total lack of ornament, and exquisite materials.*

1965 In the (black-and-white) film *Alphaville* Jean-Luc Godard refuses to follow cinematic convention: "a film is just a film—pure illusion."

1967 Jacques Derrida ("there is nothing outside the text") publishes no less than three books, all disseminating the critical theory of Deconstructionism.

1972 The Tate Gallery acquires *Equivalent VIII* by Carl Andre (made in 1966). It is a pile of bricks. He is an artist. The press and public are duly outraged.

1980~2000

Bits and Pieces
Deconstruction

Deconstruction (or Deconstructivism) is "part of a research into the dissolving limits of architecture," according to Bernard Tschumi's words at the 1988 First International Symposium on Deconstruction in London. It

The "building" at the Parc de la Villette in Paris by Bernard Tschumi has something of an early Russian Constructivist look.

is looking for "the between." According to the American architect Peter Eisenman, at the same symposium, architects who "fracture" are merely illustrative; they are not challenging any preconceptions. The ideas are borrowed from the work of French philosopher Jacques DERRIDA.

While the theory, the "new way of seeing," for architects and academics may be viewed as a decadence, it more importantly offered an alternative influence to the increasing banality of Postmodern formalism. The resulting buildings actually seem to fit the word—dismantled, fractured disassemblages, with no visual logic, no attempt at harmonious composition of façades, no pragmatic reason. For Eisenman this can be seen as a development from his abstract Formalism of the 1970s. In a critique of Eisenman's Aronoff Center at the University of

Cincinnati (1989–96), Frank O. Gehry is dismissive: "The best thing about Peter's buildings is the insane spaces he ends up with. All that other stuff, the philosophy and all, is just bullshit as far as I'm concerned."

LA FOLIE

The garden folly returns to its French roots in Bernard Tschumi's Deconstructivist work, Parc de la Villette in Paris (1984–89). Sitting at the intersections of a 328 x 328 foot (100 x 100 meter) square grid, and interrupted by existing buildings and the overlaying of pure polygons and meandering pathways, the folie, like Eisenman's houses, contains "ideas," not "functions."

Daniel Libeskind's major building is the Jewish Museum (1997), an extension to the Berlin Museum. Referred to as "between the lines" by Libeskind, the form and spatial organization of the building are derived from the history of the German-Jewish relationship in Berlin. The zigzag plan represents the continuity of history. The overlaid straight line becomes invisible where it crosses the zigzag—representative of absence. Recently Libeskind has won the competition for the extension to the Victoria and Albert Museum in London —a similarly Deconstructivist proposal that has sparked controversy.

NAMES ON THE WALL

Peter Eisenman *sees architecture as the means by which we should be shocked out of complacency at our routine existence. He inserts awkwardness and ambiguity into the built environment to open our eyes. In House VI (for* **Suzanne** *and* **Richard Frank***) one must turn sideways to enter a door, duck to descend the staircase, and negotiate dinnertime conversations around an intruding column. Perhaps unsurprisingly, Eisenman is more active as a polemicist than as an architect.*

Say What?

It's been said that Deconstruction "…has an austere sound to it which makes it some sort of sign in our timid and disabused times." Yep, and like Postmodernism, with or without a hyphen, it's just as hard to define. Jacques Derrida (1930–) would have Deconstruction allow you to ignore the boundaries keeping certain disciplines apart. So now you can play baseball and cricket in the same game. Talk architecture and Oreo cookies. Just look at the structure! The finish! The texture! And because the language of Deconstruction is so vague and contorted, you can confuse everyone by meaning something but implying something else. Cool, oh? For some reason this confusing business is called discourse, presumably to indicate the breadth of intellect required to cope with it. To be fair, the opportunity to move freely and make unusual connections can be interesting when used safely, but discourse? Don't bother: call a spade a spade instead.

Frank O. Gehry's museum for the German company Vitra. White plastered walls contrast with roofs clad in titanium zinc.

Abstract forms

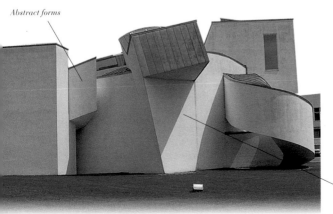

No overall harmony of composition

1982 IBM markets the world's first laser printers, which put the message swiftly and (relatively) silently on paper.

1985 The British Antarctic Survey detects a hole in the ozone layer, explaining why male architects have given up wearing suits and ties.

1989 The launching of the *Galileo* space probe, which will send back the first-ever pictures of an asteroid (1991). Most architectural historians are not sure what an asteroid is.

1990~to date

Building in Cyberspace
Virtual Worlds

The space created by our computers, can exist anywhere and is not bound by any physical or cultural context. According to Michael Benedict in Cyberspace: First Steps *(1991), the "concretization of the world we dream and think in," the "venue for our consciousness," can be whatever we want it to be. With the right software and some keyboard skills, anyone can make a complete escape from the "real" world into media-land. It is hard to imagine a world where the tangible, sensual experience is replaced by thought, a world where the body is redundant.*

> ### NAMES ON THE WALL
>
> *"I make conceptual architecture … In our office we don't make the drawings first; the first two weeks we have discussions … If we could say in words what we wanted to make, then the project would in fact already be finished … On the other hand … the most irritating thing in my view is to talk too much about architecture, because words have a very arbitrary relationship with architecture. You need to forget the words because the architecture will say it with other means."* **Jean Nouvel**, *1993*.

I ronically, the new generation of buildings, which rely on computers to aid design, have an extremely highly developed sense of the physical. The new Guggenheim Museum in Bilbao, Spain (1997), by *Frank O. GEHRY* (1929–) uses computer technology to make such surreal spaces, such stuff of dreams, "real." With no architectural paradigms, Gehry's buildings are difficult to describe. The sparkling metallic surface of the titanium cladding panels, and the building's relationship to the edge of the river, mean it has been likened to a great ocean liner.

1988 Architecture meets physics with the naming of a newly isolated carbon molecule—the buckminsterfullerene or buckyball—with geodesic dome structure.

1997 Dolly the sheep is cloned. Some wonder if she will turn out to be a wolf in sheep's cloning.

2000 In Greenwich, London, Lord Rogers oversees the opening of the controversial Millennium Dome; what's inside?

Shunning the now-commonplace software based on pure geometries of the Renaissance, Gehry designed the museum with software developed for the aerospace industry, which is based not on form but on surface. Mechanical technology that made repetition cheap is replaced by electronic technology: laser surveying and cutting equipment, and bar coding of each piece all handled by the computer, mean the unique is just as economical to produce as a series. Internally there is a logical arrangement of different-sized galleries, which are able to accommodate a wide variety of artists' works. These galleries are connected to a pivotal atrium rising up majestically through the whole height of the building.

The new Guggenheim Museum at Bilbao, by Frank Gehry, has a surreal uniqueness.

It could be argued that Bilbao achieves the ahistorical functional aims of the Modernist project by employing electronic technology and breaking down the form into primary elements in Cubist fashion. Spatially it offers a subjective physical experience —open-ended spaces, blurred edges, and unexpected places.

Looking after Number One

Back to the future. Will constant improvements in computer graphics, information control (the Internet), and bulletins on the general health of artificial intelligence (getting better as you read this) finally reduce the need to sustain a truly habitable home environment to secondary status? One sincerely hopes not, or white-painted boxes will be back in fashion. What all of this might just reintroduce is the concept of the unique. All those years ago William Morris was the craftsman's champion, but the new defenders of the faith will be the architects and manufacturers who can design and build to order, using any number of basic templates that can be articulated by a computer to suit the client. Away with the suburban home; welcome to your own, unique home, all of it prefabricated. Why exist in someone else's concept?

Looks like a computer game setting

Future Systems Footbridge at Canary Wharf, London Docklands, is designed by Jan Kaplicky.

The Great Eight

To make a listing of the greatest buildings in history is an impossible task. But it's a good after-dinner game to play for the newly architecture-literate. The eight selected here would at least give a good basis for discussion.

THE PANTHEON, ROME, A.D. C. 120
HADRIAN

This giant rotunda, 141 feet (43 meters) in diameter and 141 feet (43 meters) high, is an amazing piece of construction. Apparently simple, the wall supporting the vast dome zigzags around niches, effectively forming buttresses, and the spring line inside is a whole one-third of the height lower than the outside. The concrete dome is coffered to reduce the weight. All of this is clever, but the vast emptiness of the interior volume, lit only by the daylight through the circular opening at the top of the dome, still rates as one of architecture's most dramatic experiences.

The Pantheon in Rome, a building that combines simplicity with a monumental impressiveness.

THE CHURCH OF THE SACRED HEART, PRAGUE, 1928–33
JOZE PLECNIK (1872–1957)

An elegant simplicity of form and composition; a basilican rectangular block with clerestory windows houses the main nave space with a single, full-width tower on the west elevation. Behind the huge circular glass clockfaces, a long, slow ramp zigzags up to the bells at the top of the tower. The simple forms are embellished with stylized Classical motifs and the large, windowless areas of wall leaning as if to yield the interior are patterned with protruding bricks that distort the perspective. Plecnik studied under Wagner in Vienna, and much of his most notable work is in Ljubljana, Slovenia in the former Yugoslavia, where the nationalist culture favored his brand of regionalism.

THE ROYAL COLLEGE OF PHYSICIANS, REGENTS PARK, 1960
DENYS LASDUN (1914–)

The Royal College of Physicians is a perfect example of modern architecture. The various volumes of the building housing the different activities of the college are described by a range of structures and materials. Dark blue earthy bricks meander over the sunken conference room, and part of the public space of the building. A slim white slab raised high up on slender columns contains the library, the permanent element of the college. Only narrow slit windows in the extreme corners allow views out across the park. The heart of the building is empty apart from the staircase—the place for the procession to pass, the ritual of access to the profession.

THE MÜLLER HOUSE, VIENNA, 1930

ADOLF LOOS (1870-1933)

The cubic, rectilinear, austere exterior of the Müller House in Prague offers little clue to the intriguing spaces of the interior. The introverted, intimate spaces are interconnected—the *Raumplan*—and seem as if carved out of a solid form. Loos is as important for his extensive writings as for his built works; his major essay, published in 1908, is *Ornament and Crime*, one of architecture's most influential works.

THE WHITNEY MUSEUM OF AMERICAN ART, NEW YORK, 1963-66

MARCEL BREUER (1902-81)

Leaving his native Hungary behind, Breuer was one of the first generation of Bauhaus students, moving from painting to furniture and taking over furniture before moving on to architecture. He eventually joined Gropius as an associate professor at Harvard, following work in London for F. R. S. York and a short period in Berlin. The robust and strongly articulated forms and rich textures of raw materials at the Whitney are typical of Breuer's work.

THE KIMBELL ART MUSEUM, FORT WORTH, TEXAS, 1966-72

LOUIS KAHN (1901-74)

The Kimbell galleries in Fort Worth, Texas, consist of a series of majestic vaults that "fulfilled [Kahn's] greatest dream, defining spaces through the unification of light and structure." A series of little courtyards open to the sky interrupt the rigorous alignment of the vaults. Kahn's work stands alone; it has been linked to Brutalism due to his use of raw materials, a ruggedness of form and monumentality, and the skilful manipulation of natural light. His work is also linked to that of the Neorationalists through their shared interest in elementary forms and archetypes.

THE FORD FOUNDATION OFFICES, NEW YORK, 1963-68

KEVIN ROCHE (1922-) AND JOHN DINKELOO (1918-81)

Both of these worked for Eero Saarinen and took over the office on his death in 1961. The Ford Foundation has a sensual tactile presence, with rusty Cor-ten steel and pink granite juxtaposed with delicately detailed filigree air grilles, balustrades, and concealed lights in brass. The covered courtyard, the threshold to New York's 42d Street, is a veritable oasis of dense greenery.

NOTRE-DAME-DU-HAUT, RONCHAMP, 1950-54

LE CORBUSIER (1887-1965)

The chapel at Ronchamp, a highly specific building created in response to a particular program for a particular location, shows a refinement of the ideas in Le Corbusier's earlier work. Functional planning is combined with sculptural, curving concrete work to form some of his most beautiful spaces.

The chapel of Notre-Dame-du-Haut at Ronchamps, France, shows the features of Le Corbusier's later style in the expressive sweeping curves of the concrete roof and tower.

Techno Speak

A selection of useful terms to help you through the maze

AEDICULE
Sometimes called a tabernacle. A niche or a window framed with Classical columns and entablature.

AMBULATORY
The passage or cloister around the east end of a church behind the altar.

APSE
The usually semicircular termination of a church or chapel sanctuary.

ARCHEFORM
From archetype, it is used to mean the original model or essential or underlying form.

BAROQUE
Late Renaissance architecture, starting in Italy (17th century), characterized by disregard for the Classical language or the orders. Flamboyant and dynamic. The term comes from jewelry; Baroco, meaning rough, unrefined stones.

BAS-RELIEF
Carving in low relief on a flat background.

CABINET
French, literally closet or cabinet. Commonly used for *le cabinet de toilettes*, the toilet.

CARYATID
Column in the shape of a female figure.

CHEVET
Typical in French Gothic cathedrals, an apse with ambulatory and radiating chapels.

CLERESTORY
The upper level of the central part of a church with windows above the level of the aisles' roofs. Now commonly used to describe windows at high level.

COFFER
Recessed squares or other geometric shapes in the soffits of arches, domes, vaults, or ceilings.

COLONETTE
Little column, such as around windows.

CONSOLE
The term used for the bracket that projects to hold up the weight of a cornice or something similar. When supporting a cornice above a doorway usually called an ancone.

CORTILE
Internal courtyard usually surrounded by a colonnade.

ENCEINTE
A military term for the grounds of the fortress or castle enclosed by a wall or ditch; the enclosure.

ENTABLATURE
The cornice, frieze, and architrave, making up the area above the columns in the Classical orders.

EXPRESSIONIST
Architecture that is not imitative of a past style, and that is more than a utilitarian provision for need; a building that describes or expresses other qualities.

FLÈCHE
(from French for arrow). A thin spire, usually of timber, rising from a roof.

GEODESIC
A space frame of hexagonal shapes forming a dome.

HAMMER BEAM
Roof timber configuration where there is no other support across the space.

LOGGIA

A room that is open on one side (or more), often with columns. A kind of open balcony recessed into the façade.

MANNERIST

Applied to Renaissance architecture that subverted the rules of Classicism.

METOPE

Space between two triglyphs in Doric entablature; it may be carved or left plain.

NYMPHAEUM

Running water, greenery, and statuary—a temple of nymphs —a place for pleasure.

ORIEL WINDOW

A window that projects from the surface of the façade, projecting out on masonry. In modern domestic building, a bay window.

PEDIMENT

In Classical architecture the triangular bit of wall with sloping cornice, above the entablature. In Renaissance architecture, the same triangular piece, but also in semicircular form or with broken or open cornices on any roof end, or above a window or portico. In Gothic architecture, the gable end

PIANO NOBILE

The principal floor, a raised ground floor over a basement or first floor. It usually has a higher ceiling than other floors.

PILASTER

Rectangular projection from the surface; as if a column is embedded in the wall.

PILOTI

Columns at ground-floor level supporting the building above.

PNEUMATIC

Lightweight structures supported by air.

PORTICO

The entrance hall, vestibule, or porch with roof supported on columns on at least one side, usually on three sides.

QUOIN

From the French word for corner. Usually dressed stones of alternating size, laid at the corners of buildings.

REREDOS

The ornamental screen behind the altar, often in carved wood.

RETROCHOIR

In an important church the space behind the main altar.

RUSTICATION

Large masonry blocks often with variety of rough-textured surface and deep joints, usually at the lower level of Renaissance buildings. Rusticated blocks are sometimes used on columns and also faked in stucco.

SERLIAN WINDOW

A key element in Palladio's work, it is more usually called a Palladian or Venetian window. A window (or archway sometimes) with a central arched opening flanked by two square openings.

TRABEATED

Structure of posts (columns) and beams, in the manner of Greek buildings. The opposite of arcuated, employing arched structure.

TRIGLYPH

Block on Doric entablature separating the metopes. Two vertical grooves called glyphs in the middle and half glyphs at the edges. Without the half glyphs it is called a diglyph.

VOLUTE

The spiraling scrolled end of the Ionic capital.

ZIGGURAT

From Mesopotamian temples, used to describe stepping up and inward in pyramidical form.

Index

PHOTOGRAPHIC CREDITS

AKG: pp. 14TR, 16, 17, 18TL, 22, 45, 64, 72, 81, 86, 87, 96, 97, 103, 108, 109
Angelo Hornak Library: pp. 27, 28, 30, 44, 57TR, 75, 76, 79, 88, 111TR, 122
Arcaid: pp. 20, 23, 36, 37, 39, 40, 41, 43, 50, 51, 52, 53, 55, 56/57, 59, 66, 67, 68, 69, 70, 73, 77, 80, 82BR, 83, 91, 94TR, 95, 98, 102, 104TR, 104/105, 106, 110, 111BL, 113, 114, 116, 117, 121, 125, 126, 127C, 128, 129, 130, 132/133, 134, 137T 136/137
Axiom Photographic Agency: pp. 100BR, 101

Architectural Association: pp. 26TR, 46, 33, 35TL, 71, 107, 112, 120
Bridgeman Art Library: pp. 29, 32
J Allan Cash Ltd: pp. 61
Edifice: pp. 34, 35TR, 78, 115, 123, 135
Norman Foster & Associates: 127TL
Trip & Art Directors Photo Library: pp. 14/15, 19, 21, 25, 31, 38, 42, 47, 48, 49, 54TR, 58, 62TR, 62BL, 63, 65, 82TL, 99, 131